WELL ... ISN'T THAT INTERESTING

A Memoir

Edward M. Brady

For Dolores and Ed Brady,

the finest people to have ever set foot on this planet.

Preface

I met Ed Brady in 1998. Soon after meeting, Ed shared the story you are about to read. I've heard Ed tell this story so very many times over the 25 years that we've been together. I never tire of hearing it again.

When Ed decided to write his memoir, I became an enthusiastic cheerleader. As an artist, I have learned to "trust the process" when embarking on a creative project. Ed's slow and unfolding process to carefully recount the events and the days in which his life changed greatly impacted our relationship, for the better. Together, we weathered the emotional ups and downs, the painstaking research, the conversations, and the frustration during long stretches of time in between bursts of writing. When Ed would read a passage to me, I would inevitably burst into tears, being so filled with many emotions.

During the years Ed was writing, we had numerous philosophical conversations about the nature of the creative process, the weirdness of it, the vulnerability, the courage it takes. When Ed was ruminating and not writing per se, I would ask him, "How do you know you are not writing?"

To say I am proud of Ed doesn't begin to express my joy and appreciation for everything that led to the completion and publication of this story. I'm thankful to know and love the people you will meet in this story. I'm deeply grateful for Ed's courage and willingness to develop emotionally through the creative process in which he wove together all the threads of his history to create this memoir.

--Marian Rich

"There comes a time in every man's life, and I've had plenty of them."

--Charles Dillon Stengel

The possibility of seeing a girl naked was finally on the horizon. An upcoming five-day co-ed class trip into the nether reaches of Sussex County would certainly be eye-opening and pants tightening. Without a sister or any kissing cousins within a 50-mile radius, my everyday opportunities were few, not to mention my experiences were... well, sparse. This would be better than hitting a dinger in the bottom of the ninth. The mind raced to the point of exhaustion. The thought of seeing Yvonne or Ginny or Karen buck naked ... maybe even Mrs. McBriar, the *other* junior high Earth Science teacher. Being 13 years old, I'd be way ahead of the curve. Oh man, why couldn't I get her class? A real grown woman. A voluptuous and buxom real grown woman. Jesus, I'm getting lightheaded. Imagining the possibilities was too much to digest.

We'd be staying in log cabins with plenty of windows, all within walking distance. There was a rumor of outside showers. Man, I'd give away my Topps 1969 baseball collection for the logistics and a timetable. Think this would have happened if I decided to go to Catholic school?

Of course, this epic trip into the hinterlands would be about forestry and hiking trails in the wilderness. The alluring and intricate beauty that is nature. My square and stodgy science teacher explained why this trip should be treasured and cherished. He was animated to the point of apoplexy.

1

Imagine, setting foot on the world-renowned Appalachian Trail, he proclaimed. Yeah, right. Who gives a flying rat's ass? For the first time I would experience consecutive days away from Mom and Dad. No parents for five days. Most importantly, no parents for four nights. Oh, man. This could be better than, than … than watching Davey Johnson's deep fly ball land in Cleon Jones' mitt for the last out of the 1969 World Series. My buddies and me would pass into *coolhood.* Even though 7th Grade had a junior adjoined to its title, as in *you're just in junior high school,* this trip meant elevation into the big time. The expertise in my resume would enlarge. I mean, I did kiss Patty Adkins last summer. Even managed to feel a protrusion over her t-shirt. Actual nipple. What does that really look like?

Alas, nakedness did not come to pass on our foray into the wild on that class trip, though I did become friends with Sue O'Donnell, a well-developed tomboy, the perfect combination. Anytime she saw me, I'd get a punch in the shoulder, my first experience with foreplay. I also got a quick glimpse of Donna Pampaloni's ass as she traipsed up a steep incline. It was the first time I realized underwear came in colors.

That trip was a privilege, though I was unaware of it at the time. Hell, it was a privilege to walk out the door without getting your ass kicked. Nearly all the working-class neighborhoods in New York City were being neglected to the point of ruin, the product of white flight. South Bronx, Washington Heights, Hell's Kitchen. The loss of control and the sense of safety eroded, creating a New York City unrecognizable and foreign. My buddies' parents echoed the same refrain: we had to get away from "them." Their message was clear, without the racial epithets, although they would flow after a number of brews. Working class Irish, Germans, and Italians had to escape the "zoo."

From the Poconos to Montauk, turning rundown summer cottages into year-round homes became a booming industry for the local banks and contractors. My folks got a six-percent mortgage on a $9,100 home in the summer of '67 in Hopatcong, New Jersey. The monthly payment was around 60 bucks a month, and they were scared shitless. Some of my buddies' folks—ah hell, most of my buddies' folks—couldn't afford the fees for this five-day trip. Jesus, some of them couldn't afford the twenty-five-cent-a-week milk money. That was a damn sin. I took for granted that whatever the costs, Mom and Dad had it covered.

The decision to attend a public school had come three years earlier. In August of 1967, Mom, Dad and I had an actual semi-adult conversation, my very first grown-up meeting of the minds. The public grammar school, an eight-minute walk from our bungalow-turned-year-round house, would soon turn into the brand-new Hopatcong High School. The nearest Catholic school was 30 minutes by car, or 70 minutes by school bus. St. Adelbert's, my old school in the Bronx, was five blocks away, so this initial adult decision was a no-brainer.

It was barely a month after our exodus, and I had made quick friends. None of them were going to Catholic school, and they were all Catholic. My first semi-adult decision, the very first time where my folks actually asked for my opinion, would ultimately be my educational ruination, though my social development would go through the roof. Imagine having an actual conversation with a classmate *during class*. The chance to address teachers like a fellow human being, and not apostates from hell. Imagine, expressing oneself without fear of retribution from black-robed sadistic fiends from Hades, also known as Catholic nuns.

Though I didn't know it at the time, this was the beginning to my road of underachievement. Any chance of attending Princeton or Notre Dame went right into the shitter that very day. Therein lay the rub. Every year, it was the same refrain from my teachers: I had the gray matter and chose not to use it. In my senior year class eight years later, of the 110 students getting their worthless diplomas, my academic ranking was 127th. Yes, my GPA was that bad. Never mind that the school nearly lost its accreditation from the state, that was beside the point. I was the poster boy for indolence. Apathy and ambivalence oozed from my pores. Hell, I'd have problems getting through the doors of the local two-year college, the County College of Morris, better known as Harvard on the Highway. I was a lazy and spoiled only child, but I was gregarious and cute.

The move to this country-oasis in the summer of 1967—this designated rural hovel known as Hopatcong (that's hoe-PAT-kong, not HOP-it-cong)—was so much more about necessity than choice. It came about through dire circumstance. The location itself and the reason we emigrated to this place in the world was created through tragedy. My mom's kid brother, Jack, was killed in the Korean War back in 1953. Grandma took the two grand from the life insurance granted to all survivors of KIA's (those killed in action) and used $900 to purchase a half-acre "somewhere in Jersey" the following summer. For the next dozen years, it was through the pained efforts of my dad and maternal grandfather that the getaway bungalow morphed into our new home. Any free weekend, they would schlep out to Jersey to pour concrete, lay cinder block, saw wood. This was to be the family's sanctuary, a summer cottage, a place to breathe. It became an escape hatch. We'd leave our ground-floor, two-bedroom, rat populated, pre-pre-war stifling apartment during the summer weekends for fresh air and quiet.

5

We departed for good in July of 1967. The Melrose section of the South Bronx had turned into a god-awful hellhole. Trepidation and unease had turned into outright fear for my parents and grandparents. Puerto Ricans and Blacks were replacing the Irish, Germans and Jews. Neighborliness withered and trust evaporated. The informal nods and smiles, the simple non-verbal acknowledgements between neighbors morphed into a head down, mind your own business posture. Yes, these were cultures clashing, though it was prejudice and racism, like an invisible kryptonite, which took hold. The place where they were raised, the place where their parents were raised, was now unrecognizable and dangerous.

Moving out of the Bronx was akin to losing a limb. My mom sobbed inconsolably on the night she and my father packed up the apartment. As for the final sojourn out of the neighborhood they'd known all their lives, and the 50-mile trek out to western New Jersey the following morning, my mother, quietly sobbing, didn't say a word. She considered herself a New Yorker until her dying day.

When we got back from our G-rated five-day excursion, an essay was due that Monday. *Stokes State Forest is nestled amongst the majestic Kittatinny Mountains in Northwestern New Jersey. The scent of fir emanating through the winding trails gave off a sense of solitude and contentment. Picture postcards do no justice, that is the bounty of nature that surrounds me.*

I wrote that as a 7th Grader. The only reason I vaguely recollect the above brilliance is that I received a grade rarely achieved … an A. The real reason I got this statistical anomaly is that after class, my English teacher told me he was most impressed by my ability to place majestic and New Jersey in a coherent sentence.

It was a little sad leaving what was my first real adventure away from Mom and Dad, though I was excited to come home, knowing I'd be consuming my first digestible meal in nearly a week. Whoever made that meatloaf for three consecutive lunches should be placed before the Nuremberg judges. Without any advance knowledge, I knew that, at home on Friday night, we were having pot roast and mashed potatoes. The smell of ginger snaps baking and onions brewing amongst the drippings of heavenly gravy nearly removed the visual fantasy of a nude Ginny Morretti.

I turned up Durban Avenue, waving at smiling parents, their cars going by with my buddies firmly nestled amongst their overly excited dogs and siblings. Walking up the slight incline, the appreciation of home washed over me. Me and my buddies had mastered a week-long trip away from our familiar confines and conquered the nether reaches of the outside world. As I fixed my gaze upon a figure in the distance that seemed to be running toward me, a horn honked. I turned to see Mrs. McBriar driving a late-model

VW Bus, smiling ear to ear, wearing a white shirt knotted at the waist and mostly unbuttoned, waving and pointing at me. "See you Monday, Brady!" She always called me Brady. Jesus … my mind races.

I turned back to my trudge home where that running figure came into full view. It was my mom. Dolores Brady was running straight toward me. It was the first time I'd seen my mother running, and it would be the only time.

I think back to a Pulitzer Prize-winning photograph published in *Life,* (or was it *Look* magazine?). It was taken in July of 1973. A young woman running to meet her dad on a military base tarmac coming home from Vietnam. Her face expressive with excitement. Both arms opened to the sky. The absolute perfect shot of unfettered joy. As my mother approached me, her expression encompassed rapture, exhilaration, and relief all in one. I dropped my weathered, badly-stenciled duffel bag full of dirty laundry and broken pinecones onto the side of the road. I had barely spread my arms when this lean, slender woman, all 130 pounds of her, encased me into a full-out bear hug. How the heck did she get so strong? Though her mouth was nestled to my ear, she made an excited proclamation that was indecipherable. The scene remains vivid oh so many years later for what went through my mind. I can recall at that very moment thinking, "Ma, it was four days."

This was the first instance.

* * *

The day after Thanksgiving 1990 we spent in repose and contentment. Tammy—my wife at the time—and I loved the Turkey-Day holiday. It was so much more than those four days off. It was the Irish and Italian tight family upbringing. Imbibing and eating with no remorse or reservation. One of Tammy's and my mutual attractions was sumptuous and well-prepared meals. One of *my* main attractions to *her* was the Sophia Loren figure she developed from consuming those meals. My beautiful gal was Rubenesque and fit.

We first met in December 1980 at a disco, The Limelight on Lake Hopatcong. For years it was a burger joint known as Lenny's Pagoda. It was where I had my first part-time job attempting to be a full-time adult. I was a dishwasher and gopher peon for the short-order cooks. Years later, Lenny's kids turned it into a bargain basement Studio 54 rip-off to sell working class twenty-somethings overpriced drinks. Throughout our time together, Tammy and I attempted to outdo one another with our childhood and teenage tales of gluttonous holiday consumption.

For us, this long holiday was to celebrate the sweat and toils of our moms' and dads' labors. My voluptuous better half took after my mother-in-law when it came to the kitchen. My gorgeous 30-year-old gal was masterful beyond her years, though this Thanksgiving would belong to my mom.

Since the passing of my father in February 1985, Dolores Brady lived by herself. We spent most of the holiday with her, though we'd get to see everybody. Both of our families having migrated from the big cities to the pastoral climes of western New Jersey back in the mid 60's, we needed to take the I-80 interstate, and we had the process down. Grocery shopping on Tuesday evening. Anything my mom wanted and items she hadn't realized she needed were packed into our fridge. The pickings at her local A&P and Three-in-One deli were a tad limited. Irish soda bread didn't seem to make it past Newark. For Tammy and me, Wednesday evening brought a long, lazy dinner, though this year it was our first in our brand new, two miles from the Lincoln Tunnel, heavily mortgaged, three full-baths, sparsely laden *"…we did it, this is our place…"* home. There was a perverse pleasure in waiting until 11:00 PM, whilst a third of the metropolitan area headed out into the hinterlands traveling west.

The late Thanksgiving Eve traffic was light, making our sojourn tolerable and, dare I say, pleasurable. We pulled into 304 Durban Avenue around midnight. Mom would be backlit standing behind the screen door. I never asked her how long she stood there, waiting. She pranced down the eight, wide concrete steps my grandfather had made with cinder block, rebar and Rheingold beer cans nearly 30 years ago. Like a four-star Michelin chef bestowing upon his minions the ingredients which created the sauce of the gods, my long-deceased grandpa took great pleasure back in the 60's in instructing his only grandchild on the perfect amount of cement powder, sand and water to form an impenetrable block of sidewalk. The worn and outdated house invariably had a welcoming aura. Tammy and I were home. We were home with Mom.

The feel of the place was deepest in late 1979, coming home from the Navy. The neighborhood did not *look* small, it *was* small. The place seemed timeworn, modest. Context had changed. All which had meaning? Not so much. Spending three-and-a-half years assigned to an aircraft carrier, my core developed a form of calm disruption. I thought of my wanderlust as a teenager, going over the Delaware River when I got my driver's license so I could declare I have been to *three* states. My prism, now untethered from the bright lines of Catholicism and working-class nobility, begat a tinge of *learned malice* and odd thoughtfulness. I was denser. It was deeper than the mere passage of time. My britches were bigger. I'm glad I left the Navy. The itch to have more in my life moved me out of this place. This place was now, well … it was a place, and that was ok. The richness and comfort of this station was Mom and Dad. They were here. That gave this place meaning.

The six, seven, eight times my dad and I went out for a few belts now merge into one. The joint on Lakeside Boulevard was classy enough not to call it a joint. Bending an elbow with my father back then took on a richer meaning as I approached and then passed his age. Jesus, I miss him. The capacity I had to throw down a twenty onto the bar declaring "this is on me," gave me a brash and warm confidence. *That's alright, old man, I got this.* Seeing him snicker with a half-smile and relegate his wallet back into his olive-green work pants gave me a week of good vibes. I treasured chewing the rag with him about absolutely nothing of importance, though there was this story …

Wait, before that, another story …

My first year of Catholic school began in the fall of 1963. First grade is full of nervous excitement. Everything is new. Wearing this odd though official uniform. Meeting fellow compatriots for the new journey ahead. We are going to be in this together. Fun and teamwork. Oh man … talk about wishful thinking. Six years of age and placed into the hands of Polish Catholic nuns, women born at the turn of the century, who spoke in a form of metastasized dialect from the Austro-Hungarian Empire. It is not a stretch of the imagination to see these individuals not as emigres but refugees, who suffered humiliating and foreboding circumstances. Women choosing a path of theological study and a life-long commitment to material and sexual abstinence. Choosing may seem generous. There were not a lot of options available. These dedicated servants had escaped from the hands of Cossacks, Franz Joseph, the Czar, Nazis (probably all four), and had the misfortune of being born into hellacious and unforgiving environments. As a man now in my 60's, I'm able to discern and distinguish what these women sacrificed and experienced. As a six-year-old, all I would glean was fear and dread. The recollections of my weekends were of textbooks and theology. There is discipline, and then there is abuse. My Pollyannaish musings of comradeship turned into *survive and bear it*.

About three weeks into my sentence, aka St. Adelbert's on 155th Street, Sister (unpronounceable Polish name) led the class in morning prayers, speaking in clear *Polishhungarczechese*, the same vernacular as Linda Blair in *The Exorcist*. We rose from our knelt position, always keeping our

13

heads down in deference, and hurriedly took our splintered seats after the sister exclaimed "SEEEET!"

Mein Fuehrer looked over her flock. The white cardboard glued to her face surrounded by a heavy black ... robe? ... dress? ... couch cover? ... *(don't you ever look in the mirror?).* She glared at each of us as if we had just lifted her wallet. What was she looking for? On this particular morning, she found it.

The paramount lesson for all students was conformity. We are all the same in the eyes of God, therefore personality and independent thought was reason for execution. One of my classmates came to the stockade wearing her hair in pigtails. The sister did not so much glare at this small-for-her-age-and-ever-so-slight-little-girl as she attempted to melt the girl's brain with her eyes. After thirty seconds of staredown, she bellowed in tongues, loud enough to be heard through the ceiling. Of course, with none of us fluent in *Sanskrit,* she merely brought our level of fear to near defecation. To hell with *The Exorcist,* demonic possession exists.

My classmate began to cry. She was two desks behind me to my right. I not only heard her panicked gasps; I felt the sobs. The sister bellowed one last missive and moved up the aisle. Every nun had a wooden rosary draped down the left side of her body. The off-white cord signifying poverty and

14

sadism fell down the right side. Anytime she strode down the aisles in the classroom, the clank of her beads against our desks forewarned her craggy, wrinkled digits squeezing your ear, then tapping the desk as you attempted to write out the Ten Commandments in their proper order, while also peering over your shoulder, ready to pounce on her next meal. The black robe grazed my elbow, and I tightened my folded hands to the point of whiteness. To turn around would result in turning to stone. She blared something unintelligible, enhancing my classmates' howls.

There are events that defy description. Memories may fade with time, though there are deep-rooted recollections, with no possibility of erasure. The sounds which erupted behind me are encased in me. My First-Grade teacher took hold of each pigtail and lifted the little girl up, straight out of her desk. In what was an autonomic response, I turned my head to see the little girl raised above the nun's head, her spindly legs kicking the air. The sister backtracked down the aisle, the girl screeching and crying. Upon reaching the front of the classroom, she dropped the girl to the floor, keeping a firm grasp of her hair. It was outright panic, no … it was helplessness. No, that wasn't it. It was terror. Yes, that's it, terror encompassed the room. My 6-year-old eyes were transfixed on this small girl splayed out on the floor in the front of our classroom, with this towering black mass screaming at her and at us. This ugly and foreboding creature in black finally dragged her victim out into the hallway, her screams streaming through the now-closed door. My classmates and I sat in our tiny, splintered desks, trembling. For close to 40 years, I despised the color black, until I moved into Manhattan, where black is always *de rigueur.*

Back to that night with my dad at the bar. I don't know how we got to talking about the Bronx or school back in the day, but we'd have been in the *feeling no pain* stage of bar time. There was no particular topic or schedule when we went out for a few. Two guys shooting the shit, grateful for the time and privilege.

"Do you remember that lump on your head?"

Wow. Where did that come from? How the hell did he remember that? "Hell yeah, are you kidding? It's probably the first time I saw stars. I didn't know what hit me."

He downed a shot of Seagram's and motioned to the bartender. "I know *what* hit you. I know *who* hit you." He took a beat. "That's something ..." My dad trailed off and looked to his left, grabbed the bar towel sitting near the tap and wiped his hands. There was nothing on his hands to wipe.

In the Third Grade, I had become what one would call collegial and outgoing, a nice way of saying I never shut up. For me silence was not golden. The classroom was merely a congregation of friends and familiars, for the purpose of dialogue and opinions. Chalk it up to the only-child thing. I'd have a conversation with my Willie McCovey baseball card on how to hit Koufax, simply to keep my jaw moving. I talked to strangers incessantly. The main reason my folks never let me out of their sight was a fear of my being swept up by whomever because I was so damn trusting of everybody.

It was late May, early June in 1966. As was my norm, I was in class chattering away to a classmate, when I felt a sharp thwack to the back of my skull. All the nuns had a wedding ring on their fourth finger, making God or Jesus the record holder for bigamy. This righteous servant of the Lord implanted a concussive blow, producing stars in my eyes and the exit of oxygen from my body. She began an indecipherable tirade, though I was unable to comprehend her screams of frustration in my semi-conscious state. As tears welled in my eyes, a persistent throbbing commenced on the right side of my head. The entire class became a morgue. I felt all of my classmates' eyes upon me. In reality, they averted their eyes from any contact with our teacher for fear of getting decked.

My mom's friend, Bibby, would pick me up from the house of horrors on foot at 3:30, along with her daughter and another kid from our building. The four of us used the five-block walk to sing silly songs of brag about who had more

17

homework. Not that day. When Bibby asked about school, I was surprisingly silent. She placed her arm around my neck and asked about who the Mets were playing. This normally set me off on a twenty-minute diatribe. I didn't say a word.

As we approached the entrance to our apartment building, our superintendent, Stan, was jawing with two other men, all of them holding Rheingold beer cans. He assumed a catcher's crouch down to my level to squeeze my cheek with his stogie-stained hand. His stale cigar and beer breath, normally a reason to turn away, now seemed welcoming.

"Little Brady, what are you cryin' about?" There were now six sets of eyes fixated on my face, causing me to go into full-out blubber mode. I was embarrassed, humiliated and ashamed all at once.

"I'm sorry…" I said to no one and everyone. "I'm sorry."

"Whaddya got to be sorry about? Everything's swell. How about a sip?"

"Don't you dare!" Bibby playfully swatted his baseball cap and squatted down to look at me straight on.

"What's the matter dear? Did you get into a fight? Somebody say something not nice to you? Tell me."

At this point, I was so embarrassed and humiliated, the tears were uncontrollable. The whole scene was now

18

about losing face and looking ridiculous, not necessarily the growing lump on the right side of my skull.

"Hey, Bib, what the hell?" Stan felt a protrusion as he rubbed the top of my head. Bibby placed her hand on the exact point of impact. How did she do that? Her cupped hand engulfed the right side of my head. Her normally open face turned sour.

"What happened babe? What happened honey? Did you fall?" Her expression and her tone were foreign. Discomfort and not knowing what to do hovered over the both of us.

This may have been my first encounter with grown-up panic. In the big blackout of the previous year, there was mutual concern and discomfort, though it felt more like an impromptu block party. Everyone seemingly had a role of responsibility to play, and everyone went about their unassigned roles. Mr. Perez directed traffic. A couple of guys sat outside Ann's Bodega on the corner, checking out the customers. No electricity, it's ok. We got it under control. Now, Bibby and Stan's demeanors were different. It was not knowing what to do.

I felt a cold and wet substance on my developing lump. Stan had placed his beer can against my head. I glanced to my left to see Bibby running into our building. The other two men were muttering something about "it's" ok and "it's nothing to worry about." One of them mentioned boxing and getting worse in a ring. Stan went to one knee, holding his near-empty but cool can of Rheingold to the side of my head whilst emptying its contents.

"Ed ... woood!!"

My mother's voice could be heard a half-mile down Melrose Avenue. She'd get home from her monotonous back-office bank job about four o'clock. Noticing everyone gathered around me brought her worst instincts to bear.

"Stan, what's going on? Honey ... baby, are you ok? Is everything alright?"

"He's ok, Dor. Got a bit of a bump here. Nothin' so bad."

Mom caressed my face in her Oil-of-Olay-scented hands. She peered straight into me, passed my eyes into my medulla oblongata, the very base of my brain. It was her innate form of truth serum.

"Tell me what happened. Tell Mom what happened."

"The sister hit me with her ring because I was talking in class." Christ, she hypnotized me better than Dracula.

Bibby rushed through the building entrance, her hands outstretched, clasping a dish towel filled with half-melted ice cubes. Pushing Stan aside, she knelt down and gingerly pressed the soaked cloth to the ever-growing lump.

"Oh, God, Dolores, I don't know what ..."

"The sister punished him for speaking in class without permission. The sister's ring created this …" Mom looked at me, tears running down my cheeks, and stood up while keeping her left hand on the nape of my neck. Bibby removed her makeshift ice pack and rose to hear my mom muffle two or three sentences secretly into her ear.

"Mommy, I'm sorry I'm in trouble, I didn't …"

"Edward, how about some Bosco and a Ring Ding?" Oh man, talk about the magic words. My mother made everything phenomenal.

Normally I'd have my regal repast in the kitchen, but not this day. On this day, I got to sit in Dad's recliner and watch the *Soupy Sales Show* with nary a mention of homework. The incessant throbbing disappeared after the first Ring Ding. *This is how princes are feted. No, not princes. I am the KING of all that surrounds me. This is living.*

My father was not the introspective type. In his life, deep thought was an excuse not to get off your ass. The countless times I heard, "No one promised you a living," and "Pull yourself up by your own bootstraps," during the first 18 years of my life. No *home relief* for us.

"That day …" He paused, stared straight ahead, and sighed. "I'm going to tell you this, and don't tell your mother."

"Yeah. Sure." I took a beat. "Who did you kill?"

21

He placed the bar towel back by the taps. "You're close."

He had my undivided attention.

"That was a hot day. Miserable." The bartender hit us again. My dad downed his fifth (?) shot of Seagram's. My father was an accomplished drinker. During the Depression, his mother would garner a bushel of over-ripe apples, make four pies, and use the peels and cores to create a fruity "bathtub Calvados" for a nickel/dime a shot. This was his morning orange juice.

"Your mom had a look on her face as if somebody died. She gave me a kiss on the cheek, and I asked her who croaked. She told me what happened to you. I went into the living room, and you were in my chair, having cookies. I threw my jacket into the bedroom (he never threw any clothing anywhere) and I saw that ... lump on your head." His face reddened. My father's affect metamorphosed. For the next two minutes, I was looking at someone else.

"When I saw that lump ..." He downed half a glass of his beer. "I grabbed my wallet and keys and, without saying a word to your mother, left the house. Parking was always a pain in the ass, and the aggravation of having to find another parking spot added to my ..." He turned in his stool and looked at me straight on. "I double-parked in front of the school. A kid finally opened the door after I banged on it. I went up the stairs and found three of them standing outside of the principal's office." It was the only time he ever stepped foot in the place. "I asked if any of them were in charge. One of them stepped forward and said her name was Sister Alda and she was in charge. She asked who I was and *What are you doing here?* The sides of his mouth turned upward, and he poked me in the chest with three fingers. *'What are you doing here?* That did me in. I looked at her dead-on and said 'My name is Ed Brady. If you or any of you old bitches ever lay a hand on my kid, I'm coming back here and throwing you out the fucking window.'"

It was the first time I heard my father utter that particular word. He went on to say he brought home baked goods every day for a week after my no-contest bout with Sister *Unmentionable*. It was the last time a nun ever touched me.

Jesus, I miss him.

* * *

Thanksgiving of 1990 was heartening and congenial. Mom, Tammy and I enjoyed each other's company, which made for a splendid day and a kick-ass repast. The entire day was slow, easy and rich. The setting was classic Americana. I was splayed out on the ancient and well-broken-in Sears and

23

Roebucks couch, half asleep and half observing the Detroit Lions losing to whomever, while the two most important women in my life prepared our feast. Late in the afternoon, we'd bid serenity adieu and wend our way to the in-laws' log cabin for dessert. Yes, that is correct … Lydia and Tony's log cabin was situated on umpteen acres, where the deer strolled up to the windows. Tammy's three older sisters, their husbands, and our seven nieces and nephews would be in attendance. In all fairness, I went for Grandma Nicolina's cookies. Jesus … those damned cookies. Homemade Italian butter cookies made from absolute scratch. Never had anything like them before or since.

This holiday had a deeper meaning. It was a hard-earned respite for us. When we had finished our gleeful Tuesday evening shopping spree, there was a message from Mom. As I dialed her number, I knew what was coming. She had three appointments at the Roxbury Medical Group with three different doctors, one being an oncologist. Finding out there is cancer in your family is, at the very least, very unsettling and profoundly heartbreaking at its epoch. Uh … yeah. Right. I'm attempting to be eloquent. Cancer is the bitch of all fucks. Man, from my earliest memories, the hushed conversations I overheard about sickness, and cancer in particular, were all laden with fear and despair. It was a scourge with no enemies. The disease was everywhere.

Somehow, it seemed like a rite of passage. Baptism, communion, confirmation, marriage, cancer. Fraternal grandfather I never met, lung cancer. Maternal grandfather, John Baldock, a permanent seasonal groundskeeper employed by the NY Giants at the Polo Grounds—who, without knowing, passed on to me not only cement mixing recipes but an endearing and lifelong passion for baseball at the earliest possible stage of my comprehension—lung cancer. My father's mother, "Goom," who I rarely saw, lung cancer. My mother's mom, Bunny, who lived with us the last 14 years of her life, and who had a Salem in her mouth from the moment she arose until the moment she laid her head down at night, lung cancer. My father died of emphysema at 60, which is a fancier way of saying goddamn lung cancer. Now my mother. Smoked from her early teens. They all smoked, though I would call it ingesting feces. She read to me from her copious notes what the oncologist said ... she had acquired small oat cell carcinoma. Acquired? How the hell does one acquire cancer? Small ... oat ... cell ... carcinoma. I thought of cereal. It sounded like some bastardized form of Cheerios.

Yet, there was not a word of regret, nor was there a smidgen of *woe is me* from Mrs. Dolores Theresa Brady, originally and, according to her, exclusively from the South Bronx. We're talking stoicism beyond all realms. It wasn't just living through the Depression and the Second World War that gave this now 64-year-old Irish looker an inner emotional strength that General Patton could only strive for. There was this resolve of determination and focused vivacity not found in many women of her generation. My mother had a tall way of standing. Dignified. A class act. Upon initial introduction, more than a few people would intimate her background must have been of higher standing or even nobility. Welcoming without being forward. Tasteful, though not in any way pretentious. Understand that she admired educated and purposeful women yet looked askance at the single-minded politics of a Gloria Steinem. Of course women are treated poorly. All women need to be recognized and respected. Watching Steinem on *David Susskind*, my mother stated ever so succinctly to the television, "Why aren't you inviting men along for your *revolution*?" She'd look at me matter-of-factly, then with distain add, "Isn't there strength in numbers?" It wasn't the possibility of becoming a lead secretary or an overworked glorified office manager that drew her interest. There was a desire, a burning need to create for her family (meaning me) options that weren't available to her or my father, though conveying this doctrine into the skull of her laissez-fair son was no small task.

In the nearly six years since my father had passed, my mother tried on numerous occasions to quit the damn coffin nails, only to be rebuffed time after time. Shortly before my dad died, they both tried hypnosis for Christ sakes. Nothing took. They both told stories of how the movie stars, generals—anyone who was anybody back in the day—had a cigarette in their hands. I would bite my tongue when the "If Johnny jumped off the Brooklyn Bridge, would you?" line entered my frontal lobe. On the few occasions when I voiced my smug and condescending concern on consuming 60-80 cigarettes a day, the look I would receive is what Southerners would call the "bless your heart" response. I would mind my own business, though when we left her early Friday morning, the look and the hug we both gave her conveyed, *we're here for you. We will always be here for you.*

The next day, Tammy and I settled into a restful coexistence, not giving a damn what the weekend would bring. When the phone rang after dinner that Friday night, we would have normally let it go to the answering machine. Besides, after hearing my mom's diagnosis, we were emotionally spent. Yet this was the first night she was alone with the knowledge of her diagnosis. Still, the odds of her calling after eight were remote. My mother was proudly self-reliant. I could hear the constant repetition of "no one promised you a living," "create your own path," "nothing will be handed to you." This now rang hollow. There is toughness and there is compassion. We would be there for her.

Tammy answered. I picked up the holiday edition of our newly subscribed *Architectural Digest*. We were now bigtime homeowners, so why the hell not?

"I'm afraid she's not here. May I ask who's calling?" I wasn't paying attention to the call. I was half-admiring all the items we would never be able to afford, half asleep as I rifled through the Rococo godawful excuse for furnishings.

"I'm sorry, no. May I ask who's calling?"

I paused my interior decorating search and listened to an odd line of inquiries.

"No ma'am. It is not. Are you from the Bronx?" I sat up. I made eye contact with Tammy, who looked puzzled and gave me a "I don't know/what the hell" grimace. I shrugged back.

I wondered if a distant cousin from the Bronx got wind of the news. No. How the hell could they? Even if they did, Mom was close to the vest on all matters. She'd never divulge any unhappy news without a federal warrant and an Act of Congress.

"No, ma'am. I'm sorry, I'm unable to give that to you." I finally mouthed "Who is it?" She placed her hand over the mouthpiece and whispered, "I don't know what's going …" then stood up straight and stated with a slight tone of conviction, "I'm sorry but I'm unable to provide that." The back and forth went on for another minute. She took a breath, then calmly, with a bit of reservation, stated to the caller, "Miss, her son is sitting right here. Why don't I give you to him?" As Tammy handed me the phone, she gave me a new look I had not seen in our ten years together. It was a look of concerned weirdness.

"Good evening, this is Ed. How are you?"

There was audible breathing coming through the receiver. Not quite a gasp, more like regaining one's breath after climbing a flight of stairs.

"Hi ... um ... (breath) ... oh ... Hello!"

"How are you?"

"Hello." There is a long pause. "I'm Mary."

"Good evening, Mary. May I help you?"

"Oh ... yes ... I'm looking for Mrs. Dolores Brady..." Dead air for eight or ten seconds. "Yes." Six seconds ...

"Yes ..." I answer.

A few more seconds, and then a resounding "YES. Mrs. Dolores T. Brady."

Dolores *T.* Brady? What the hell is going on?

"Ma'am, I'm afraid she is not here."

From here, the memory is not exact. There was some back and forth about the 1950s, the Bronx, mentions of her family past and present. All the while, Tammy and I were exchanging inquisitive looks: is she in need of money, is she a stalker, is she an old girlfriend of my dad's? Even if any of this was in the ballpark, why was she calling us? Whoever this was, she was taking great pains to maneuver without moving. I got to the point where this was enough mystery. I interrupted her.

"Ma'am, I'm sorry. If you would be so kind as to tell me who you are and then we could move forward …"

There are times in all our lives that adhere to our senses. The first kiss. A well-earned promotion. The imperceptible yet sentient event moving you and your family from working class to middle class. Matters which seem banal and outright ordinary become an indelible etching in the mind. What I heard next from Mary became the focal point in my life. I felt Mary brace herself on the other end of the line. I swear I could feel it.

"WELL …" she stopped. I remained silent.

"Well… I'm simply going to say this straightforward." She took a beat. "Well … on March 2nd, 1957, I gave birth to a seven-pound, two-ounce boy …"

Let's pause here for a moment.

How often does our mind race to the point of incomprehensibility? The thoughts and scenarios careening as a blur, like standing on an interstate overpass. The inability to identify one car from another. All motion and chaos and no time to laze or to gather a thought. Yet at this moment, at this precise moment, my immediate reaction was to repeat to Tammy everything Mary said. This may have been a gut reaction. It needed to sound real. This was the only present, cognitive thought. This is what is happening right now. This person is telling me I came from her. I was created by her. Time is being stilted. Time is bending. She is now speaking to someone for the first time in her life who she lost. Or was it given up, or was it taken away from her nearly 34 years ago? As a numbers guy, the 3/2/1957 date and stated birth weight were ringing in the background. March 2nd, 1957. How the hell does she know my birthday? Because she was there, dummy? No. Wait. Texas. Orphanage. Older brothers. Teaneck. Looking for me all these years. Sisters and a brother. Did she say Teaneck? Teaneck, New Jersey? That's 15-20 minutes from us. The Foundling Church, no, hospital, no, Catholic something of nuns in Manhattan. My mind was blank and yet it was racing.

For a moment I became self-conscious of my breathing. My regurgitation of Mary's chronicle of events paused. My brain lifted its foot off the gas, and I inhaled air and expanded my chest to the point where my eyes became saucers. I exhaled. Tammy reached out and caressed my thigh with a look that says, *are you going to faint?* The feeling was similar to being roused from the couch after an unexpected

31

nap. I nodded no and maybe half-grinned like a stroke patient. An actual thought finally became speech.

"Mary ..." that's all I said. Mary. Then silence. No, not silence. It seemed more like dead air. It was the mind and the body needing a break. A pause. A literal breather.

"Well ... Mary ..." Here again, the memory is a fog. Was there a mention of a husband? Another reference of Texas? She was in the Coast Guard? No, the Navy. Jesus, she was in the Navy? There was more than a feeling now of indecipherable rapidity. The brakes needed to be applied.

"May I ask for your address? Would you mind if I had your phone number?"

"Oh, yes. Of course. Please, thank you."

"Please allow me to get a pen."

"YES. Uh ... oh ... take your time, Michael."

Michael. Where did that come from? How the hell does she know my middle name?

Writing down the info, the realization of closeness sank in. Teaneck. Union City. The Bronx. Is this really happening? The call was coming to a close.

"Well, Mary ... I'll be in touch." Well, Mary ... I'll be in touch? Those words stuck and repeated themselves in my mind like a bad song.

"Oh my, yes, thank you. Thank you, you've ... you ever so much. Goodbye, my dear."

32

"Goodbye."

My thumb hit the off button. For a deep moment I zeroed in on how badly my thumbnail and the surrounding cuticle were chewed to the point of soreness. Did that occur during the conversation? I had always bitten my nails, but it became a revelation that my finger looked chewed up. Jesus, my fingers looked like hell.

"Ed ..." Oh Christ, Tammy. She had taken a position on the floor, legs underneath her looking up at me, and then, without losing eye contact, rose to sit on one of the custom-made chairs we purchased from a firm recommended in *Architectural Digest*.

"You know ... I think it's true."

"You think it's true." It hit me I no longer needed to parrot everything. I was off the phone.

"I think it's true," she came back. Seriously. Why? She began to explain how my mother would not discuss her pregnancy. Tammy had three older sisters-in-law, with seven kids. Tammy reveled in visiting her sisters and being with their kids. There were times she immersed herself in all matters of birthing and mothering. Before we met, it was also a way to get the hell out of the house and away from my overbearing and pain-in-the-ass father-in-law.

"But dear," I came back, "my mother would never discuss anything having to do with s-e-x." That's correct.

Dolores would spell out the word and not pronounce it. We're talking the product of 1930s Catholic school and a father who beat her senseless for dating a "greasy overambitious Italian." Apparently, Italians were over-sexed. Who knew?

A few years back, I hooked up her cable box to get HBO and Showtime without charge. I was a big George Carlin fan. I made the mistake of suggesting one of his specials. It was the last time she turned on either of those channels, and she didn't talk to me for a week. This was a prim, proper woman. OK, reserved and more than a tad prudish. This was not someone willing to openly discuss water breaking and placentas.

Tammy continued on how there were no pictures of her during her pregnancy. Why would anyone photograph a woman with child? Anytime the conversation turned towards childbearing, my mother would listen and politely nod. I thought of my mother-in-law and wondered if I had seen any photos of her with child? Understand, I wasn't being defensive, and neither of us took a side. We weren't interested in debate points. We then paused and started on Mary Hauptman. How the hell did she get to us? Why now? What kind of ulterior motive might there be? This wasn't a scam. Why be so forthcoming with your own info? She didn't ask for anything in particular. How the hell did she obtain all this background on Dolores *T.* Brady, yet contact us? Could there be a mistake? I thought of Cary Grant's mistaken identity in *North by Northwest.* Bad info. I don't know. Damn, what the hell is going on?

We normally would put on the idiot box until we got sleepy. Not tonight. Though neither of us had come to a conclusion, or even an educated guess on what had just transpired, we were anxiously curious and challenged. We might be able to help her with whatever she was attempting to accomplish.

Volunteering my time had begun to grow larger with each passing year. For the past four years, I had been reading to a gentleman who was legally blind every other Saturday morning. The activity of me reaching out to The Lighthouse coincided with the passing of my dad. I never put the two together. The subconscious at work. Every other Saturday, it was a rich and relaxing two-and-a half hours with a wiser and worldly gentleman. Giving of time and energy was a natural move. Maybe, maybe this was something akin to that. This poor woman got a hold of some bad info. We could help. Then …

Well, then … Jesus, this was so weird. The few notes I jotted down during the conversation were eerily prescient and on the money. Living in the Bronx and close to where we resided. The Catholicism running through the process. *Giving*

35

me over to the nuns at the hospital. That stuck with me. How do you say no in 1957 to Sister Augustine-Mary-Teresa-Catherine-Mary-Bithia-Florence-Satan-Mary whatever? The absoluteness in her voice. Her case was damn convincing.

Tammy and I tossed around a scenario where she was a Gloria Vanderbilt type who was seeking a lost heir to her trillion-dollar estate.

"Well, it looks like we are headed to the East Side of Manhattan."

"Oh yeah, sure."

"The *Upper* East Side of Manhattan."

"How about an apartment in the Marais? How about downtown Rome?"

"I'll call Nelson Doubleday and Fred Wilpon and take the Mets off their hands. Then I'll call Frank Lloyd Wright's office to build a decent stadium."

After the silly pipedreams, we thought of Mary Hauptman. Here was a person putting herself out into the ether to find someone she had lost. What must it be like to be looking far and wide for a child you gave up? No, a child who was taken away in her most vulnerable moments. How could she have gotten so far off the path? Doesn't she have help? Did I ask if she was married/widowed/divorced? The call went so fast. Did she mention someone? I remember sisters and brothers. Family in Texas and/or here. Were they her siblings? I began on the path of "This poor thing was all by herself slogging through a painful and draining process that might have no end." I went out to the car and got the beat-up Rand McNally map of New Jersey out of the glove compartment. She was 25 minutes away, less with no traffic. Do I call and invite myself? That's too much. What kind of mental stability are we dealing with, and how do I proceed? It's not that she was manic, though there was something in her speech I couldn't describe. Call it a sultry, constrained hysteria. Alright, let it go. Fall asleep. Breathe. Take a deep breath. I finally fell off and slept well that night.

The following morning, Tammy was already downstairs puttering and had poured OJ and cranberry juice into a glass. This was unusual. It was the first move I would execute every morning, and there was only so much cranberry juice added to keep the mix perfect. She did it flawlessly.

"So."

"Yeah, so." We glanced at each other and chuckled. "So, what's new?" I asked. She got serious. "You gotta do something. I don't know what she intimated, but you have to do something."

I took a beat. "I gotta call her."

"The woman?" she said.

"No," I shot back, "I gotta call Mom."

"Mom? Why get her involved? This could be someone that … that … I dunno …"

"What are you thinking? I'm open to suggestions."

"If any of this is right, why did she call us?"

"If any of this is right, why would anybody act in any way? Who the hell knows?"

"That's true."

We sat in silence for three minutes. I decided I'd call my mother.

"What are you going to tell her?"

"Nothing. I'll go see her."

"You're gonna drive back out to Hopatcong?"

"That's where she lives, dear."

"Stop with the smartass. You gonna go see her?"

At that moment I visualized my father sitting across the table. Though we had the same name, I was not junior. His middle name was Thomas. My middle name was Michael. My dad had a quick wit and a straightforward way of being. Street smart and one hell of an intuition. He read someone within 30-40 seconds of meeting them. Always smelled bullshit and would keep his distance from it for the simple reason that he didn't want to waste his time. Life was too damn short. His most admirable characteristic was facing problems head on. He said to me, the adult way to succeed was to face anything right in the eyes. It was the way to be

38

respectful and decent to all involved. "You are going to come into contact with people and situations in the Navy that need sincerity and direct answers, especially with assholes. Always be direct and decent." I decided to see my mother. I told Tammy this was best done solo.

I called Mom to say I'd be in the neighborhood and would stop by. She was a bit surprised but buoyant about an unexpected visit. I didn't go over any dialogue with Tammy. I didn't see a need, though this had to be broached. Look at this straight on. I would talk to my mom and help this poor woman, Mary, clear up her confusion and get her on the right track. It was the decent thing to do. It was the giving thing to do.

Though the drive out is a blur, perceptions and conclusions bounced around my head. The mind wasn't racing so much as it was idling at 60 miles per hour. For the first time in my life, I became conscious of my breathing. I pulled into 304 Durban Avenue. I walked up the stairs as my mom opened the screen door.

"Where's Tammy?" she asked. She assumed it would be the both of us. I gave her a peck on the cheek.

"Let's sit down."

I owed my mother directness and maturity, but from the time I've been able to get a laugh, I've been sarcastic. Sarcasm has been my *raison d'etre* since, well, since forever.

There is a skillset involved in implementing the right amount of fact and skewed silliness in order to achieve the desired eyeroll, huffed groan, half smile. When invoked with the proper timing, there is an invisible connection between you and the target, allowing a jaded intimacy you both share in the moment. It gets you remembered. I had the luxury and privilege of being inane and silly at any opportunity. More than habit, it was comfortable. No matter the situation, no matter who I was with, I had the ability to mock and tease to gain acceptance and to ease the strain. Being an only child, I always felt the need to make everyone comfortable. It was paramount.

Not now. Not this time.

Dolores Brady was the older child and only daughter of Agnes and John Baldock, two unlettered yet savvy working-class Irish-Germans from the Bronx. Money wasn't hard to come by, there was none. Grandma a seamstress, Grandpa a laborer. There was more than a rumor John did "running" for Dutch Schultz's mob. Whether that meant the numbers or a wheel man, I never found out. He copped work wherever it could be found. When the Depression hit, it was simply another day in the Baldock household. Finding enough to eat was standard operating procedure. Who gave a damn what a bunch of *hündinnen* did downtown? We would take care of our own. This is the mindset drilled into little

40

Dolores Theresa. It sure as hell was burned into my *amygdala*. You make your own way. No *home relief* in this house.

So, Mom hit the books. Read everything. This was her escape, the way to find a semblance of control. Anytime I broached her childhood or adolescence, it was hard for her to salvage memory. She always came back to her reading and schoolwork. I didn't get the vibe of anything ugly. Simply, it was damn hard times. Best we forget and move on.

No matter how difficult her childhood, the virtue anyone would prescribe to my mother, should anyone be placed under oath, was her honesty … honesty to the point of numbness. When I inquired about the Easter Bunny or Santa Claus, she'd direct me to my father. She was unwilling to go along with lying about Santa Claus.

Though she was soft spoken and slight of build, she would not tolerate rudeness. Succinct and direct, placing herself in tense situations, she would more than make her case with a modest tone and clear diction, with more than a hint of moral superiority. Dolores forgave outward sleights, and Dolores would always remember those sleights.

Dining at my in-laws one Sunday, Tammy's father blurted out an untoward remark to my mother-in-law. This resulted in an embarrassing and uncomfortable state of affairs for everyone. My mother inhaled with purpose, placed both of her hands on the dining room table, turned her head toward Tony, and said nothing. After three seconds, my father-in-law went to the bathroom. As he mumbled under his breath, my mother gave me a glance. It's remarkable how much can be relayed with a momentary look:

I miss your father.

Same here.

How I wish he were here.

Same here.

Can you believe what you just heard?

Yeah, I know.

How does Lydia put up with that?

You got me …

I'm proud of you.

Back at ya …

All of that in a glance. Christ, I miss that woman.

How many thousands of times had I walked into this house without a care in the world, free of any worry or responsibility? Slipping into my room to watch the Mets lose, lounging on my bed, drifting, thinking of nothing, awaiting my dinner like a half-assed prince. The only child who got everything. I didn't have the "world owed me a living" mentality. That would have been slapped right out of me. It was more of, *well, that's how it is.* This is the norm. I never got the sense I was putting a strain on my mom or my dad. They were happy to give. They wanted to give. It was a compulsion

42

to give to the baby. Little Eddie. Little Brady. Little Boo-Boo. It was their ordained duty to look out for me. This gift would be nurtured *ad nauseum*. What mattered beyond any other need or want, no matter my age, whatever might be transpiring in their world, everything was geared toward the baby.

We reached the living room and sat down in those worn-out, cushioned chairs. The peering look of warmth and concerned puzzlement was across my mom's face. "Is everything all right, dear?" she asked, placing both of her hands behind her upper thighs as she sat, sliding them down to her knees to keep her threadbare yet pristine housecoat straight underneath her. The woman never had a wrinkle on her.

"Well," I said. I looked right at my mom in a new, foreign way. I looked at her with longing, a kind of contemplative "aww, gee" and "thank you," which I could see was not registering. The gaze lasted long enough for her to ask, "What's going on, Ed?" I muttered something like "okay" or "alright."

"I've got a helluva story to tell you." At first I fell into the cadence that was oh so recognizable and banal, speaking in a sing-song manner reserved for a 6-year-old regurgitating *Green Eggs and Ham*. Then I took a breath and transformed into a 33-year-old man with something serious on his mind.

This was not going to be the cute smartass. While I looked directly into my mother's blue eyes, I was talking behind her eyes. It was a wholehearted effort to look into her as an x-ray would look for fissures in bone. I was attempting to speak to her soul. While I concentrated on my mother's eyes, I had little emotion. I wanted to relay the content on yesterday's phone call with no extraneous info, and especially no hint of judgement. Seriousness was not my forte, and yet I felt myself being General George C. Marshall giving instructive and concise intelligence to his one-woman battalion.

I told her everything. The conversation was more of a lecture. Just the facts, ma'am. Information being given to a class of one. I made an attempt to deepen and punch my delivery in areas of import, like the Bronx and the Catholic Archdiocese. Being direct and succinct is not all it's cracked up to be. The briefing came to a close. I sat back in the chair with my legs open, arms collapsed onto the oaken armrests. I didn't want to look like a physician giving bad news, yet my demeanor probably gave off a *thank God I got that out* feeling. Now I looked at my mom completely. Her demeanor and the expression on her face were nondescript. She had not moved in her chair. After listening intently, and without a hint of alarm or concern, she folded her hands into her lap, looked away while pursing her lower lip, then adjusted her gaze directly toward me.

"Well, isn't that interesting?"

Isn't that interesting. That was it. No inflection. No other comment. No sense of urgency or discomfort. A matter-of-fact response. Straightforward and pointed. She was polite and taking it in as if I described the removal of groceries from a brown bag.

Okay, now what? Yogi Berra once said when you come to a fork in a road, take it. This is exactly how I felt.

Any attempt at further conversation seemed feeble. How the hell do you sit in front of your mother and tell her that last night you spoke to a woman claiming to be your mother? (Or is it *my* mother?) There was mention of volunteering my time and this person may be in need of assistance. Is there a way to help without hurt? How did this person receive all this info? My mom was being direct and distant. I pictured my father. In the deepest recesses, I heard him: Don't BS, be straight, and always be decent. There may be a playbook for this scenario, but where?

There was another fleeting thought: I recalled stating to my buddy, Bill Peterson, when we were out on one of our late-night benders how my mom was one tough broad. Here is a woman who lived through the Depression, WW II, had a hard-assed German father who once beat the hell out of her for dating an Italian, lost her kid brother in Korea *after* the armistice was announced, nursed that same dying father for months so he could die in his own bed, then took care of her unresponsive and near catatonic mother for 14 years. And did I mention she raised me and took care of my father? Whatever the hell was going on, Dolores Brady appraised and organized any circumstance with aplomb and dignity.

"Mom, am I adopted?" I fixed into her eyes.

There was a beat, maybe a beat and a half. She adjusted slightly in her chair, bringing her left arm across her chest, grabbed her right elbow and leaned toward me for emphasis.

"No."

That's what I needed to hear. Not a particular result, mind you, but rather a definitive "this is what is happening."

Ok. All settled. I exhaled with authority. This is where we're at. This poor woman, Mary, got led astray. However she got to this place and time, it was a mistake. A well-meaning yet ill-informed person got a hold of the wrong individual. It happens.

Most importantly, my mother never lied.

From the time I was stationed on an aircraft carrier, I was aware of the pace at which we process data. Though speed and quickness were imperative, the repetition of your assignments broke it down to a point of banality. General quarters meant get to your post, set up your gear, be in position. Focus. Over and over again. It became innate and

46

mundane. You thought of it as much as you thought about breathing. There was no fucking around. It was serious business. This is how you progressed, or your buddy was dead. After two weeks of drills, I surmised this allowed nearly every sailor to enhance his capabilities and bring even more to the table. Familiarity created confidence. You owned your task. I knew what to do.

Though there was a sense of *OK, that's taken care of,* a surge of obligation washed over me. This poor woman, Mary, needed the straight dope. No reason to leave her hanging.

I got up and said, "Mom, I'm sorry for all this. You can see why I wanted to talk in person."

Mom answered authoritatively, "Of course. Heaven knows what transpired for her."

I walked over to her so she needn't get up. I bent down, kissed her cheek, and extended my arm to mildly rub between her shoulder blades. "Tammy and I had nothing planned today. This woman gave me a Teaneck address. I may give her a call and stop by." This was not entirely altruistic, as I thought of how Mary received ...

"You're gonna go see her?" My mom blurted the sentence out in such a fashion as to bring back her Bronx syntax. This was a rarity. Ever since the move to New Jersey, she took pride in annunciation, if only to distinguish herself from the yokels.

47

"Why not? This will be my Thanksgiving good deed."

I located my jacket on the far end of the couch. My back was turned away from my mother. I walked the four steps and bent down to remove my scarf from the inside of my jacket.

"Are you going to go see her?"

I learned the phrase *pregnant pause* maybe in high school, or maybe I heard it on a PBS special. This moment placed an indelible mark on my psyche. This instant in time is ingrained. When my mother repeated that phrase, "Are you going to go see her?" this time in the King's English, what came from me was unintentional. It was kneejerk, an autonomic response. I lulled for the briefest moment and said under my breath "Oh shit." For the next hour I'd be on autopilot.

My facial expression did not waver. I stayed focused, only I wasn't sure what the hell I was focusing on. Walking back toward my mother, I slung the scarf around me and placed one arm inside the jacket. I touched her with my uncovered arm and gave her a quick peck on her cheek while stating I'd call her later. I exited, making sure both doors were shut tight. Halfway to the car, I heard the screen door open. Didn't I purposely force the damn thing closed? I looked up to see my mother. I know I didn't forget anything. She never looked out after I left. She always, always made a point of saying goodbye inside the house before anyone left. The act of speaking to the back of someone was rude, déclassé.

"Are you going to go see her?"

As I started the car, I made a point of not looking up. She was there at the door as I backed out of the driveway. She was there when I turned onto the road. The longer she lingered, I felt more and more. I mean I just *felt*. No describing of the emotions. Were they emotions? What exactly was I feeling? Whatever it was, there was a lot of it.

Our minds race, even when we are in repose. A quadrillion thoughts in femtoseconds. Is there a car behind me? Will that dog run out into the road? I've got 47 invoices to send out this Tuesday. Why is my ass so itchy? Don't the Jets play the Steelers tomorrow? Is that person I spoke to yesterday the reason I exist?

The drive back to Union City doesn't seem to have happened. I was there. Now I'm here. As I got out of the car, my movement turned into slow motion. Looking at our townhouse, the visual of our old apartment house in the South Bronx came into eerie focus. Ann's Bodega on the corner. Eddie Eckhart's liquor store across the street. The hint of gas from the Sinclair station. I looked at the keys in my hand. It hit me that I never had keys to our old apartment house. Somebody else always had keys. Of course not, I was 6. Why the hell did I need keys? I hear myself talking out loud

… to myself. I banged the palm of my hand to the side of my head, not realizing my keys were in that hand, giving me a decent-size gash above my right ear. I picked up the fallen keys, stood erect, and said out loud, "Relax, dickhead."

"So … how is she? What did she say? What did you say? How do you feel?" Tammy flung open the door the way our nieces ripped open Christmas wrapping. She placed both of her hands on my chest and gave me a long kiss. Slipping off my shoes and hurling my coat onto the banister, all I could muster was "Jesus." We both went into the living room and plopped ourselves on to our new, deep, overpriced, lush couch and looked at each other. "You better give me more than Jesus. My God, your ear is bleeding." Placing some paper towel over my self-inflicted wound, we moved over to the dining room table. I'll bleed on the oak.

"I gotta call Mary." That's what I said. I gotta call Mary. This is what needed to be done. I have to solve, complete, get into whatever the hell is going on. I gave Tammy a hackneyed synopsis of what happened. The thrice mentioned, "Are you going to go see her?" was the main gist I hammered home. This became the basis of thought of all else, the annoying jingle you're unable to dismiss. This was not the simple cue we see or feel in everyday conversation, the basic facial expression any 3-year-old could discern. It was becoming clear the process was muddied. This was the jolt,

the unevenness, the skewing of *what I knew to be true*. Jesus …
this could land. This could be happening. What the fuck is
going on?

The call to Mary in Teaneck didn't register. It was a
task which was needed in order to do a more important task.
I politely yet authoritatively stated to her I'd be there in 30
minutes. There was impassioned glee in her response. "I so
can't wait to see you, dear." The "dear" hung in the air. It
sounded just like my mother. Yet again, Tammy was on the
sidelines, waiting. I didn't want her to be alone, yet it
somehow seemed like her duty to stand by. After I hung up,
Tammy and I didn't say anything. The aura and the mood
changed to … I don't know. The both of us were in *I don't
know* land. Without direct knowledge or understanding, a
change was taking place, though it somehow seemed like a
change where we had a say. We had landed in *Unawaresville*, a
place Rand McNally couldn't find. I put on my coat as I
opened the door. Tammy placed her forearm on my shoulder
and kissed me on the cheek with longing. It might have been
the first time I experienced longing, so how the hell would I
know what longing felt like? She looked into me without
words. This was a first. I half smiled and said, "I'll see you
soon."

* * *

PUBLIC HEARING

before

Assembly Institutions, Health & Welfare Committee

ON

Assembly, No. 2051

(Adoption)

Held:
December 9, 1981
Assembly Chamber
State House
Trenton, New Jersey

MEMBER OF COMMITTEE PRESENT:

Assemblyman George J. Orlowski *(sic)* (Chairman)

ALSO:

John D. Kohler, Research Associate

Office of Legislative Services

Aide to Assembly Institutions, Health and Welfare Committee

******

(forwarding to page 57)

Assemblyman Ostowski: Thank you. Mary Hauptman. Mary, are you speaking for yourself, or for an organization?

Mary Hauptman: I am speaking for myself.

Assemblyman Ostowski: All right. Do you want to give us your name, Mary?

Mrs. Hauptman: I am Mary Hauptman. I am a mother. I am also a daughter. I was told my mother died when I was a baby and I grew up missing her all these years. I can only imagine how I would feel if at any time I were to find out that she hadn't died, but was still living. I would be furious at those who would deceived me, of course, only for my own good – my own good, or their presumed own good?

How can it be good not to know? "Know the truth and the

truth shall make you free." I have always believed this and I have lived it. My husband and I have five children. I have always told them: "I will never lie to you. If you ask me, I will tell you the truth, but make sure you are ready for the answer." I cannot protect my children from hurt in life. I can only be there when they need me. I do not own my children. They are free to come and go, to seek information on all things or not, as they so choose. But they do have a choice; adoptees do not. That's why we are here.

We are talking about adults. Adult is defined in the New Webster Dictionary as, "relating to full strength." I think we all try to raise our children so that by the time they reach 21, they are full strength. If they aren't, we are still there for them if they need us.

There should be no fear here. Adoptees wanting to know their birthparents are no more leaving their adopting parents than is a person leaving their natural parents when they marry. It is adding, not subtracting. As we gain in knowledge in life, we grow. If we try to shut ourselves, or our family, in, we wither and weaken. Our society is strengthened by adults who have a firm sense of heritage.

Do you who sit here on the Committee realize how fortunate you are? Has it ever occurred to you how secure you are to know that your grandmother come to the United States by way of Canada and that your father's brothers are in Massachusetts, New York, Illinois, and California? The family stories about how your great grandfather would wake up with snow on his blanket because it had drifted in the cracks in the attic where he and his *[word missing here]* had to sleep may not seem very important to you, but they are always nice to know. We all have vivid imaginations when it comes to thinking the worst. If I didn't know my parents, I would wonder: were they murderers? Did they try to drown me when I was born? Or, did a boy and a girl love each other so much that they threw caution to the wind and suffered ever after for it?

Are we trying to protect adults from possible hurt, or are we really punishing former sexual behavior? Please don't protect my husband and me from our child – our first born. I want our son to know that we did love him and that we did what we thought was best for him. He has four sisters and a brother that would love to know him. Allow him to legally have that information if he so chooses. Thank you.

* * *

Teaneck, New Jersey is a suburb about 30 minutes from the George Washington Bridge, meaning about three hours during the morning rush. This clear, crisp late autumn Saturday brought no traffic and no hassle. Driving up to see Mary, my mind created scenarios ranging from posh to penal. The poor thing must be alone and desperate. What does she need? What could we provide? What does she expect us to do? Is there an estate involved? Has she done time? How the hell did she choose us? No, wait, not right. How the hell did she find us? I realized I was driving halfway on the shoulder of the road. *Wake up, moron. Snap out of it.*

The neighborhood was nice, familiar and pedestrian. I turned onto Ogden Avenue. I was looking for the number and passed the house intentionally. I still don't know why I did that. I made a U-turn and pulled up at the curb. I didn't want to pull into the driveway. That somehow seemed rude.

Closing the car door, I took care not to slam it. It was the middle of the afternoon. What the hell was I worried about? I paused to look at the house. Tudor design? Attached garage. Brown leaves rustled on the rock-garden lawn. I was acting like a half-assed appraiser. What the hell was I doing? I approached the front door and took a breath. I knocked on the screen door. No, I rang the bell. Probably did both. There is a noise a screen door makes when you open the inside door in a rush, a slight whoosh alerting you that you're about to be greeted. I took a half step back when the screen door opened.

The woman in front of me was gorgeous. I was unable to garner another thought when I heard "May I hug you?" There was no processing. It was autopilot. I stood before the threshold, letting the hourglass figure in front of me step back and allow my entrance. I stepped into the house.

There are greetings, there are hugs, and then there are embraces. The woman enveloped me in such a way that I'm unable to justify in words. I simply can't. I'll leave it at that.

I held her in a way that I believed was more consoling than comforting, yet soft enough not to seem rude. As she pulled away, I focused on her face. She was fair skinned, light blonde, airy yet traveled. Her eyes disappeared into her face. Experienced. Really well put together. Christ, she was a babe.

We sat down in the living room and talked, with the discussion geared toward family. There were photographs on the wall, the kind of set-up showing people at different ages. They were all good-looking brunettes. Was she a modeling agent? She had three daughters. No. She had three girls close in age and a daughter a few years later and a son a year later. Five kids. Ok. Five children.

Mary leaned toward me. "Do you have any children?" she asked.

"No, ma'am." She leaned back with reservation. I probably said it with too much conviction and purpose.

"Oh, I see."

I didn't mean to throw her. I got defensive and said we had seven nieces and nephews and loved them dearly. I always loved being with kids, understanding that they would be exiting with those who brought them.

There were snapshots throughout the room. Grade school and high school shots of all the kids. There was one painting above the long couch. It looked like her and a man with a moustache. I wasn't paying attention to the décor, and yet I was taking everything in. All around me was background fodder. I was focused on Mary. It hit me how nicely she was dressed. Was she going out? Her make-up was nearly impeccable. This is a good-looking woman. Why is she alone?

She asked about my wife, then suddenly exclaimed "Oh, my dear, I haven't offered you anything? What would you like? I can…"

"No, no please. I'm fine, ma'am. I'm fine."

She folded her hands onto her lap and leaned toward me as if to make a proposition. "Please call me …" and she trailed off. She had her lips pursed in such a way as to make an *m* sound, then struggled to say "Mary." She realized, and she saw I realized, she was about to say Mom. It was the first moment of discomfort. I thought, *no problem*.

I quickly asked, "So how's your family?" She started with her oldest, Alice. Lived on Long Island with Mike and two kids. Bernice was in Texas with Ken and three kids. Carol was in Texas with Brad. Two kids. Why the hell were two of them in Texas? Are they originally from there? No, they are from the Bronx, I think. Diane was married (engaged?) and in Jersey. Eddie attended Rutgers. (Eddie … her son's name was Ed?). Was everybody out of the house? She raised five kids by herself? What did she do for a living? Does she have a boyfriend? Who's the guy in the painting? Where the hell am I? Focus!

Mary was explaining her life in a way which seemed disjointed and curious. Coming up to New York in the 50's, being in the Navy. She had three older brothers, and with their father needing to work, they spent a significant amount

59

of time in an orphanage. Her dad was "mostly away" and needed to work. "Being the youngest and a girl was very hard, but I loved my brothers." Ok, that's good. Varying and unpleasant experiences with her stepmother. "She was jealous. She was jealous." I listened with intent, though my ability to process meaning seemed lost. I was on a couch listening to a woman I did not know saying things that might be relevant to me and others. It was so goddamn weird.

A noise came up from the basement. Oh, we are not alone. It somehow gave me comfort. Somebody else is here. Somehow the situation called for more company. Ok, that's fine. I'll meet one of her children.

As the door opened, a robust older man emerged. He was around Mary's age and was sporting a full moustache. His eyes were deep. With only a glance, there was a lot going on. As he closed the basement door, I rose to meet him.

"Oh, yes, I'm sorry. Allow me. This is my husband, Irving Hauptman," Mary said.

"Good afternoon, sir. How are you?"

"How are you?" he asked.

"I'm well, thank you," I said. He nodded.

I returned to the couch and Mary began anew about something in the Bronx. There were maybe three, four lines of dialogue when she gestured toward the gentleman still standing by the basement entrance. "And your father ..."

I cut her off.

"Wait." My face must have contorted to a point of rare form. The gentleman standing by the staircase seemed a bit thrown by my expression.

"Wait a minute ... you mean to tell me ... you mean ... you mean you're my..."

* * *

Being an only child, I sometimes pondered how nice it would have been to have someone to bounce off thoughts and ideas with, or to simply chew the fat on why Ed Kranepool was better than Joe Pepitone. To have a peer would've sorta been cool, I guess. All my buddies had siblings. Ted had a much older sister, but he still had a sister. Danny had a kid brother. Jose had an older brother and two kid sisters. Fitz had an older and younger brother, then got another brother. Still, it was a lot cooler being the center of everything. No competition. I was the all-encompassing entity. No worries about being interrupted. No concerns about waiting for the bathroom. Every movement I made, every word I uttered was of the utmost importance. Unencumbered, no waiting, all was like an EZ-Pass Lane. The *baby* got everything he wanted.

Though it was a rare occurrence, any time my folks mixed it up verbally about money, the neighbors, my indifference to school, *money*, I'd interject with a smartass comment or question. I wanted both of them to have … nice. No problems or difficulties. Each of them had enough bullshit at work. Inserting myself helped to ease the strain. One day, when their back-and-forth became testy, I decided to perform my half-assed Kissinger persona.

"You know, Mom, I don't look like you or Dad. I sure don't look like Grandma. I don't look like anybody."

"What do you mean? Stop being silly. Of course you look like us."

Aha, an opening.

"No, c'mon …"

"Don't you mean, 'come on, dear'? And please, lower your voice." Raising my voice forced them to lower theirs.

"OK, yes, but really … where is the resemblance? Your hair color is different, my eyes are green, and you guys have blue eyes. You're thin. Dad is … um …"

"Dad is what?" He bellowed without turning in my direction. He was ready to pounce on any description bordering on fat.

"Yeah, well, Dad is … robust."

He let out a laugh. "Fine choice of words." He lifted his mug of Michelob. "To being healthy and robust." Mom

62

nodded in my direction with a crooked smile, acknowledging my quick turn of phrase.

"You look like Jackie," my grandmother said.

Oh my God, Grandma joined the conversation.

My maternal grandmother, Agnes Baldock, rarely opined. Reserved to the edge of indifference, Grandma's arsenal of speech consisted of good morning, how was your school day, and goodnight. Now she was speaking, and before her third *Rye Presbyterian*. My mother's mom was joining the conversation with an actual complete sentence. She was listening to what was being said and espousing an opinion. Someone alert the media.

My mom froze for a moment, then turned toward the living room. "You think so, Mom?"

"Of course," Grandma said. "Look at those full lips, look at that wonderful profile."

"Yeah, Jackie. You do look like him." Dad lifted his pen off of his route book, pointing it at me with a knowing nod. "He does from the side. Doesn't he, babe?"

Mom gave me the once over. "There is … more than a resemblance. Yes. Why … hmmm … look at the cheek bones." Within three minutes they all turned into forensic anthropologists.

"Dor, why not show him some pictures?" Grandma never called Mom Dolores.

Jackie, as my dad had declared, was the uncle I never met. Very little of him or about him was mentioned, due to the nature of his passing, at least in front of me. The reason was simple: nothing negative in front of the baby. The mere thought of war and death was too much to take, too much to ask. Subjection to anything besides sweetness and comfort would be bad parenting, which is why this conversation was unique, for the mere mention of my uncle, and his name brought distress heaped upon guilt piled onto unfathomable loss. This is the reason I had never seen photographs of my uncle, not even baby pictures.

I did have one etched memory. At a relative's birthday party, my Aunt Edna made a side comment to my dad about the day of my uncle's wake. She recalled the undertaker opening 20 minutes early. The line of visitors to see his open coffin went halfway down the city block. My dad touched her arm and placed his index finger against his lips. He didn't want his wife or in-laws to hear a word. Nearly two decades after his death, it was too damn painful. Uncle Jack Baldock was the apple of everyone's eye.

My mom paused her meal prep and said to no one in particular, "Let's get the album."

Dad stopped his route book computations. "Are you sure, babe?"

She placed the dishtowel upon the counter, wiped away a tear, and took a breath. "I'll get it."

"NO," my father snapped, then caught himself. "I'll … I'll get it, babe."

Grandma concurred. "Do you know where it is, Eddie?"

"I got an idea. There's a box …" He trailed off, got up from his recliner, and walked toward the staircase with the pull-down ladder leading to the attic.

All of a sudden, a pall came over the house. Mom's mood shifted from custodial to depressed. Grandma looked out the window, searching for something that wasn't there. I was confused and a bit worried. What the hell is going on?

Dad pulled the cord for the attic stairs. The springs gave off a jarring clank. They never got oiled. It was my folks' alarm bell. No way in hell was I to go up into the attic without their knowledge. Dad carefully climbed the unvarnished pine stairs. The sole light was a bulb hanging from one of the rafters with a long string that, when yanked, gave off a dim light shrouded in dust and cobwebs.

Mom audibly exhaled, checked the oven temperature, wiped her hands down the side of her housecoat, and walked to the side of the ladder. "Eddie …? Be careful. Do you know where …"

"It's alright." A long and somewhat deliberate pause ensued. I looked at my mom as she tilted her head toward the attic opening, staring at nothing. I glimpsed Grandma, continuing her search for something out the window. The movement of boxes and the creeks of dry plywood rattled through the ceiling. It was weird to hear noises coming from above.

"I. Got. It."

It wasn't a satisfied *Eureka!* It was more resignation and necessity. I heard the box sliding, being pushed along the ground and toward the ladder. Dad knelt down on one knee, beginning his descent with the grace of Buzz Aldrin leaving the lunar module. Halfway down, he reached for an old carboard box from A&P. (Oh God, please, Dad, don't tell the A&P joke. "Did you hear? Shoprite and A&P are going to merge. It will be called Shop & Pee.")

Mom went into the kitchen to dampen paper towels. Grandma continued her thousand-yard stare, not acknowledging my dad as he gingerly descended the creaky stairs and placed the box on the floor of her bedroom. He half-clapped his hands to remove the attic dust and closed the folding stairs. As I stepped towards Grandma's bedroom to peruse the now-unhidden treasures, Dad straightened his arm to grasp my shoulder. "Let Mom clean it off."

"I'll do it, Mom. Let me ..."

"Your mom will take care of it. Sit down."

My father's stern tone caught me off guard. I knew not to question. I sat down.

Looking over my shoulder, I saw my mother kneel down and wipe away the dust. I saw her shoulders heave once, twice. Her sniffles caused my grandmother to bow her head, her chin touching her chest. Mom is treating this old, warped box with both disdain *and* reverence. Dad retrieved an old beach towel and unfurled the worn cloth onto the middle of the living room floor, then delicately set the freshly dusted, aged cardboard box onto the towel for all to see.

Mom collected herself and came into the living room, her breathing discernible and long. She took a slug of her *Rye Presbyterian* and took a knee next to the box.

"Edward," she called my name without looking at me, which was unusual, "Please get the dishtowel."

I sprang off the couch, Grandma snapped out of her trance, and said "Is it there, dear? The yearbook and Fort Knox journal are together ..."

"Yes, I know, Mom, I packed it."

I saw my dad give his mother-in-law a wide-eyed death stare, as in *don't say another damn word.*

"Here's the towel, Mom."

"Please spread it out on the TV tray."

She lifted a number of items from the box, placing both of her hands underneath, cupped in a way so her wrists and fingertips were touching the material. My dad reached out from his recliner to run his hand down the middle of my mom's back. Though they adored one another, outward displays of affection were few and far between. The emergence of a sad smile somehow straightened her spine.

"Please take a look at these, dear. They are … well …" She stood up, extended her hand to caress my cheek, and kissed my hairline. "These are photos of your Uncle Jackie. This is your uncle."

The anxious curiosity turned into reluctance. I don't know. A sacredness, some kind of code was being broached. I'm trespassing. It's not ok to be here, but you can take a look. For the first time, I was unsure and confused in front of the three people I loved and admired and adored. I didn't know what to do.

"Pull out the photograph, Edward." Grandma fixed her gaze onto the TV tray. "See how handsome my Jackie is there? Take a look at your uncle."

The old 8x10 picture frame was half covered in cloth. My hands firmly caressed its sides, allowing the rag to slide off. Then, there he was, in dress uniform. Side cap, private insignia, smiling and proud. PFC Jack Baldock. For me, the name was merely an inscription on a headstone, and now here he was. My face opened. The smile was contagious. Everybody beamed. Jesus, what a rollercoaster.

"Your smile and his are exactly the same. The spitting image! Yeah ..." Dad was adamant that I concur.

Grandma nodded until her glasses slipped off her face. Mom looked out the kitchen window and declared, "This is not the way it should be." She turned to me with a forced smile and said, "I love you more than anything."

Dad left the photograph on the table and took the box into their bedroom. We had dinner in near silence.

This was the second instance.

* * *

I couldn't get it out. I couldn't say it. I stood there for what seemed to be an hour and a half. It was four seconds. The gentleman at the staircase nodded his head—down, up, and down again. He was confirming Mary's statement. Holy son-of-a-bitch. It's possible. Christ almighty. This is more than feasible. For the first time in my life, I was standing in the same space with the two people responsible for my existence.

"Okay."

That's what I could muster. That's it. Okay.

All of us have instances where we say to ourselves, damn I should have said *blah, blah, blah*. Why the hell didn't I think of—fill in the blank. Why the hell didn't I say …?

"Okay" seemed like the only comeback. It was the only response that made sense. Simple acknowledgement conveyed in a didactic literal form, like Hal in *2001: A Space Odyssey*. Message received.

I sat back down on the couch. I hadn't realized I was still standing. I looked at Mary. Her expression had changed to a forced smile and a strained look, like she wasn't getting something. There may have been some type of disappointment, unease. The script changed. The movement of time shifted. A new act started without the Intermission.

I wasn't in a state of shock, just lost. I needed to pull over onto the shoulder and look at the map. My internal itinerary was gone.

"Are you sure I can't get you anything, dear?"

Yeah. I'd like a barrel of Jack Daniels.

I didn't say that. I held back.

"No, thank you, I'm fine." That I did say, and it was a lie. This was the first moment when I fell into a negative field of reference. A little ticked off. A lot confused. Comprehension, control of time and space were missing. Now the questions raged. All was open to interpretation. There was nothing beneath my feet.

"Well, dear." Mary's voice brought me back. Her eyes disappeared into her face.

"Yes, well …" I needed a habit with which I was familiar, a form of self-preservation. I pulled out *the only child who gets along with everybody.* Gregarious and pleasant was the way to go. "So, yes, well … the both of you are off today?"

Brilliant, asshole. It's the Saturday after Thanksgiving. Did you think they were coal miners?

"I'm a project engineer. I work from home," stated Irving. He was uncomfortable. Welcome to the club. "Where do you, um … what do you do?"

"I'm a telecom analyst in Manhattan. I work for Dun & Bradstreet."

"Ohhh … that's wonderful. A law firm."

"No ma'am. It's a Fortune 50 company. They handle …" My voice trailed off.

As my brain attempted to garner layman's terms to explain what Dun & Bradstreet did, Dolores came into sharp focus. When I landed the job in '87, I laid out to her in great detail how I was in their research and development arm, working closely with programmers and engineers. It didn't matter that I was a glorified billing clerk. I was white collar. My mother was proud as punch. Her boy was amongst sharp people doing interesting work in technical research. She'd asked about the company, their position in the financial industry, and the opportunities for my professional growth. When I told her my boss was a woman, she pleasantly and whimsically inquired "Well, how do you feel about that?" There was a concerted interest in what I was pursuing and how it fit into the grander scheme that was Tammy & Ed. Now, sitting in Teaneck, NJ, looking at Mary, there was an instant-replay aspect. Do I begin to explain in the same way as I did with Dolores? Is this person interested in what I'm doing and where I'm going? This is not a consultation with a career counselor. I'm repeating this to my … what, who?

"Dun & Bradstreet, that's an old company," Irving said. I got the sense he needed to be heard.

"It is," I concurred. "Back to the mid-nineteenth century."

"Wow!" Mary wanted back in. She giggled and smiled the width of the room. She nodded with enough nervous energy to bring her out of and back down into her chair. I saw her wanting to be part of the dialogue, yet not knowing what was spoken and how to speak. Irving moved into the living room and sat down at the end of the couch to my left. As his body settled into the fabric, even though not a sound came out of him, I felt weight being lifted off of him and out of the room, a palpable exhale. The man was uncomfortable and somehow annoyed. The way he looked at his wife was …

odd. I sure as hell did not want to be the cause of that discomfort. This was my cue.

"Well … I want to thank the both of you for allowing me to stop by …" I rose from the couch, my body turned towards Irving. My father told me when you leave anyone's home, you say your last goodbye to the lady of the house. Where the hell he got that from, or who set up those guidelines, were irrelevant. This is how a guest exits a house. I stepped toward Irving, and Mary clenched my right tricep, the way you grab someone from stepping out into traffic. I quickly turned, as if I had a choice, and her face was inches from mine.

"I can't tell you how lovely it was to have you here, my dear. Thank you."

"Thank you, Mary. It was a real pleasure to meet you. Thank you for seeing me on such short notice."

"Now we'll see one another often. Your wife, too … I'd love to meet her."

"Yes, Tammy."

"Tammy. Isn't that lovely. Tammy."

She placed her hand on my face and gave me a hug. I graciously smiled and turned back toward Irving. I extended my hand to his already outstretched arm. There was a glint in his dark brown eyes. Was that emotion or sheer relief in my departure? We exchanged a firm handshake.

73

"Thank you for taking the time to see us."

"Oh, of course. It was my pleasure."

I peered at the oil painting of the two of them. It wasn't an exact likeness, but it was them. It hit me at that moment that they were married. Mary had said as much earlier in the conversation, though it somehow didn't register.

I got to the front door, opened it, and turned back into the living room.

"Well, thanks again." I paused for maybe five seconds. I looked back at Mary, then Irving, Mary and then Irving again. "I'll be in touch."

I opened the screen door. Mary placed one of her hands on the door and reached out to rub her other hand down my back as I crossed the threshold. I made a point of walking straight to the car without turning back. It somehow would have seemed anticlimactic. I took pains not to trip on anything or make any irregular motions. As I sat down in the car, I heard the screen door and then the inside door close. I sat in my car in other-worldly silence.

A minute passed, maybe two. I sat there. Nothing. I was consciously incoherent, out of it. Loopy without the narcotic. I was never one for dope. The idea of ingesting, inhaling, smoking, shooting some kind of—what, alternative entity into your being so you could be out of it for the sake of being out of it? Didn't make a helluva lot of sense—that, and if my father found out, I'd be walking with a limp. Somehow, drinking was OK, not just that it was legal, but there was a community aspect to the activity. When you got high doing all that other crap, *you* got high to the point of incoherence. There was an isolating aspect, a "stay away from me" stance. Having a couple of cold ones was a social event, a way to be with others. The topic of discussion was immaterial. Girls, teachers, work, family. Why the Mets couldn't keep their players out of trouble. The back-and-forth, the riffing off of each other. The company was reassuring, grounding. Gregariousness begat friendships. *We* were in this messy, fucked up world. It was a team effort.

I got jolted. Something hit me. My god, Tammy. Damn, is that what it's like to be high? I have to get to Tammy. I have to gather my senses. Don't attempt to think about what occurred. For right now, just get home.

I drove down the block, put on my right signal and came to a stop sign. There was a honk of a horn behind me. I was stopped at the corner for three, four minutes. I was in never-never land. I turned onto the main road and pulled over to the shoulder, allowing the guy behind me to pass. I was still stoned. *OK, now what? Is there a plan?* Yeah, get to Tammy.

I made a wrong turn onto I-95 and ended up on the Turnpike. At least I was headed in the right direction. I needed familiarity. My head, my stoned, half-baked head required more room to maneuver. I needed the leeway of an eight-lane highway. I needed to sober up.

As I turned off the working-class city street in Union City, and through the open gates of our faux-pastoral complex, there was a recognition of oddness, a type of other-worldly game being played at my expense. It was hard to focus. Our new triplex in this brand-new facility that was our shining moment of personal and professional achievement now seemed weirdly foreign. My internal compass had lost its magnetism.

Our parking spots were located right in front of our place. One of the advantages of being an initial investor in St. Michael's Walk was getting first dibs on all of the perks a new complex has to offer. Though we owned one car, we received two parking spots, assuring the car would never get dinged. I turned off the ignition and sat in the car. As I gazed at our new home, the first pang of—well, let's call it doubt—crept into my psyche. Doubt ... and concern.

I had stopped attending church in junior high. My father worked most Sundays, though he'd be home in time for noon mass. The grind of him getting home, jumping into the shower, dressing appropriately and schlepping to hear a boring priest had outlived its usefulness. We didn't become heathens. It was practicality, and I sure as hell didn't mind.

Besides, being a righteous and giving servant of God was not exclusive to one day a week. The sabbath day didn't have to be Sunday. I got into my most animated debate on this subject in Catholic school with my 4th Grade teacher, Mrs. Franco. She was my first human instructor. A person who dressed as my mom would dress. An actual relatable mortal. My insistence on proof that Sunday is the day to profess allegiance to the Almighty was my first adamant stance against an adult. I didn't see that anywhere in Ecclesiastes. All this profound defiance got me was an additional 45 minutes of theology homework. Lesson learned. That was my last debate. The thought of God reigning over all—all knowing, all everything, in everyone's business. For me it was a matter of practicality. If we're in your image, let us do the free will thing. To screw up is to learn, right? Talk about helicopter parenting. Leave us alone. Except, of course, if we need something. Then it's time to place a call. Times are tough, bring in Mom and Dad, or the Almighty.

As I sat in our car looking at our place, the thought of a cosmic joke emerged. Not so much penance as being used in some weird play for a reserved audience of one. *OK, God, what's the deal? Do I owe you? Did I do something horrific? Is this some sort of universal leveling out, spreading the grief around, are you a guilt-ridden Socialist? What ...?*

As I got out of the car, I stretched, as if a distance runner preparing for a race. Tammy was not anxiously awaiting this arrival. The front door did not fly open. I reached the first stair to our front door, turned around to look at the surroundings. I knew where I was. The *looking* was reassuring.

This second coming home had a deep and serious meaning. Tammy and I looked at each other the way a physician looks at a patient when he is about to deliver crucial information.

"Holy Christ. This is unreal."

"Tell me." Feeling her against me, her smell. She had just gotten out of the shower. Christ, she felt fantastic. "Start from the beginning."

It was important to be clear and direct. I needed Tammy to fully comprehend what had just transpired. The thought occurred to me that she might not *get* what she thought she was getting. I'm an Irishman from the South Bronx and western New Jersey. Edward Michael John Brady. No, I'm a-something-else from the Bronx .... or Texas ... or Teaneck. *Does it matter? Yeah, it does. No, it shouldn't. Focus, Ed. Tell her what went down. Be precise. No bullshit.*

"I get the sense Irving didn't want to be there. Poor guy was uncomfortable as hell. She seemed to be all over the place. I couldn't get a grasp on her. Nervous and excited.

Very pretty. Talking to her was interesting. And yet, I dunno, I felt bad for her. She was so nervous. Guess I would be, too. Convincing as hell."

"How many children do they have?"

"Five." We looked at each other. We'd been together for ten years. Both of us got the gaze of *I know what you're thinking.*

"Six?" I said with an upward lilt. It's nice to know your beloved is on the same page.

"I gotta call my mom. This was too damn convincing. Dolores has to hear this."

"What are you going to say?"

"I'll go see her."

"Again?"

"You think this should be done over the phone?"

"No, you're right. This ... this, whatever this is ... has to be done face to face. You have to go."

There are thousands of ways to describe unique situations, things that occur to you that stay with you a lifetime. You can become laden with *adverb disease* in your zeal to convey what was the most incredible happening in your life. Then, there are those instances where silence is king. Oratory is superfluous. It is mere noise. Being silently present is all that matters.

Three-nine-eight, zero-two-seven-six. Dialed it a thousand times. It's a thing you'll always remember and never give a second thought. Same as Ludlow five-seven-nine-nine-nine. That was our number in the Bronx. Why do I remember it? The indelible impression isn't the number, it's what you hear and how you hear on the other end of the line. On this day, when my mom picked up the phone, she was gasping for breath. All that transpired in these last hours now had no discernible value. My mother was in a place never before visited. My mom was in trouble. What kicked in for me was my concern for her well-being. A woman who prided herself on control and decorum was now indecipherable. *I'll be right there, Mom.* I said it five, six times. *I'll be right there. Don't worry. I'm coming.* I finally got an OK and she hung up.

"My God, oh dear Jesus!" Tammy became nervous, maybe a bit frightened.

For the third time in how many hours, I left Tammy in an emotional state of what, I don't know. I left once again. I had to get to my mom.

I got there in 30 minutes. How the hell I didn't get a ticket is beyond me. I ran out of the car without turning off the ignition. As I raced up the stairs, the screen door flew open. My mother collapsed into my arms. I said nothing. She was sobbing uncontrollably. Good Christ, she was shaking. I attempted to steer her into the living room, and she enveloped me. For the second time in these last couple of hours, I was hugged where words would be meaningless. Comfort, fear, anxiety, relief, radiated through my clothing. It was all encompassed with love and "thank God you're *heredness.*" (I just made up a word. That's what it felt like.)

My left arm around her waist guided my mom towards a chair in the living room. Her left hand was filled with overused wet tissues that had disintegrated into an orb of mush. In the seven, eight minutes of our embrace our eyes had not met. As my mother collapsed onto the furniture, my arms stayed braced around her waist, bringing me astride to her, one knee onto the shag carpet. Engulfed by the worn Gimbels department store cushions, she was now stable. I removed the gelatinous mass of Kleenex and substituted them with four new tissues. Her head was bowed onto her chest, sobbing but no longer heaving. I rose from the floor, placed both of my hands on her damp cheeks and kissed the top of her head. I quickly headed to the kitchen sink and grabbed a glassful of tepid water. I placed the water on the TV tray and squatted in front of her like a catcher, both of my legs encompassing her. Placing my hand on top of her knees, she began to raise her head.

When my father died at the age of 60 in February 1985, it had been sudden. The death certificate read *emphysema/ coronary thrombosis*, though the cause was eating

81

three packs a day for more than four decades and working six days a week. Dolores and Ed were Dolores and Ed for 43 years. He had been retired from bread delivery for nearly three years, but he would continue to rise at three/four in the morning until his dying day. Seeing him come home in his green work pants, and that jacket with the Silvercup patch sewn above the left pocket, he looked like a sergeant coming home from the trenches, also known as the Bowery and the South Bronx. Every weekday before my mom left for her innocuous and mundane position at the bank, she made sure to have the TV tray set up with a clean ashtray, a coaster, an opened, fresh pack of Salems, a clean napkin for his false teeth, and there were at least two beer mugs in the freezer. To this day, coming home on a hot day and having a cold brew poured into a frosty mug is one of life's absolute pleasures. Manna from heaven.

My God, how the mind works. What was coming into focus was the last day of my father's wake. It is custom for everyone to say goodbye before the mortician closes the casket. After kneeling or simply peering at the deceased, the last to view or comment are the closest family members. My father, the mortician, me and my mom were amongst the two dozen flower arrangements and empty chairs. As I peered down at my dad, in a crisp white shirt and a pristine dark blue jacket, I thought of Shea Stadium. We attended one game a year. He'd swap shifts to get a free Sunday. Sitting next to him, in those field-level three-dollar-and-fifty-cent box seats, having more than a few sips of his beer, seeing him rise and respond when we finally scored a run. The smile coming over my face made my cheeks stretch to perpetuity. I was looking at the deceased body of one of the finest human beings to set foot on the earth.

I wanted my mom to have privacy with her beloved. These were the last moments she would have with her soulmate. I turned away from my dad and embraced Mom, assuring her all would be fine. As I reached the doorway, I turned back for one last glance at my parents, together. As Dolores leaned into the casket, her shoulders began to heave. She spread her arms, mumbled, gasped for breath, and collapsed onto my father, her head pressed onto his chest below his chin. I lowered my head and passed through the doorway. I heard "Oh Eddie, please take me with you." That gesture was the most out-of-control moment of my mother's life. Until now.

Nearly ten minutes had passed since my arrival. Neither of us had spoken a word.

Dolores raised her head so that our eyes would finally meet. The eyelids blinked for control and poise. Drawing an open-mouthed deep breath, a modest, guttural moan joined a slight smile. Though her eyes were red and swollen with tears,

I saw her recover and come back to the now. *She's ok. Thank God.* I needed to see that smile. My emotional state decreased to DEFCON 3. The both of us were ok.

I stood up from my catcher's crouch, taking pains to walk backwards towards a chair, not losing eye contact. I sat back, and it dawned on me I was smiling. *Why the hell am I smiling?* This wasn't a happy time, though it wasn't a sad time. It was a transformative time. *I'm changing. The both of us are changing.* I gazed at my mom as she wiped away the moisture from her reddened face. At the same time, a gentle and encompassing—oh hell, I don't know, a spirit, an aura— enveloped the room. It was different, somewhat foreign, and yet congenial. We were sitting in a 35-year-old dwelling that had been a bungalow, which was turned into a summer house, and now was the year-long permanent residence of Mrs. Dolores Brady, 304 Durban Avenue, Hopatcong, New Jersey. It was two days after Thanksgiving 1990, and everything had just changed.

"I can't believe I'm telling you this ..."

Those were the words that straightened my spine. It was like the captain of the ship coming into your workspace as you sprang to attention. It was like hearing the outfielder yelling "I got it," calling you off the ball. My mother was going to tell me *the story of my life.*

She started with Dad.

Edward Thomas Brady was not one to mince words. He was born on August 2nd, or August 4th, or sometime in the first week of August 1924. As my mother would state ever-so delicately, her mother-in-law wasn't one for paperwork, though my fraternal grandmother was most adept at making bathtub gin. I once asked Grandma (she preferred *Goom*) when Dad was born, and she replied "In the middle of the summer. What difference does it make?"

Dad received that gene in spades. He also had this innate ability to size up anyone within 45 seconds of shaking their hand. Street smarts, never forgetting a face, intuition. There was a keen sense of the other. Again, he smelled bullshit a mile away. My mother always took pains to say how charming and collegial her beloved Irishman was to everyone he met. Except for Richard Nixon, ("That lowlife would lie to his mother for a nickel"), he never spoke ill of anyone. He would engage a person, assess their finest quality, and commend them for it. Though he had only two years of high school, the manner in which he absorbed a conversation, the way he received and challenged a speaker's ideas, was professorial and yet welcoming. I mean, who doesn't like to talk about what they're good at? For all who encountered him, there was comfort in conversing with my father.

"Your father loved children. He glowed amongst them. Having a family was everything to him, and me. There

85

really wasn't anything more than raising a family, keeping them safe, and giving them all we could." A deep breath seemed to lift her head up, allowing her to wipe the moisture from her neck. It's nearly six years since his passing, and dear God, how she misses him. "Two babies, that's what we thought … two children." She ceased rubbing the tops of her thighs with clenched fists. "Not three. Three is an odd number." (*So is one.* I kept my mouth shut.) "There was the thought of four, although … well …" Her left hand moved with a soft one-two motion in front of her face, as if conducting an ensemble. It was a cryptic reference to money. It meant the lack of money, though she would never state that outright. It would be a slap to Dad. "This would be our job, it would be … our mission. This was the reason we were here. My God, he cherished the idea of giving our kids the kind of childhood neither one of us had. To give joy. To be responsible for the giving of that joy. A real childhood …"

She sat back in her chair, eyes widening and looking straight ahead, speaking in a firmer tone. "The both of us saw what life did to us, what it did to people we knew and people we loved. The harshness, the ignominies all people faced. Now there should be discipline and respect. Always respect. But mostly … foremost … we will protect our children. We will treasure them like no one else." There was a long pause. "He reveled in being with the *kinder*."

Mom possessed that same passion. She doted over her friends' kids. Even after they had reached well into their 30's and 40's, they all addressed her as Aunt Dolores with reverence. The idea of calling her by her first name alone would be sacrilegious. A huge hug would always accompany any greeting. The color came back to her face as she described feeding and clothing all of these beautiful babies. Motherhood is the highest calling anyone can attain.

"Then came the news." She clenched her fists, tapped her thighs, and placed her arms on the armrests. "We were unable to have children. We were physically unable to have children."

It is my belief this was the first time she ever said it out loud. I never inquired as to why or how. It was none of my business. After that pronouncement, she seemed sturdier. Her posture was returning. Chin perpendicular to the floor. The shoulders went back. She took a sip of water and rearranged herself. She placed the tissues from her hand onto the TV tray. The wan expression on her face was replaced with the matter-of-fact look of a physician, or a thesis advisor who is about to explain the meaning of everything.

It was a number of years before they finally broached the possibility of adoption. To acknowledge that option was to somehow resign yourself to defeat. It was not until the death of her brother in Korea in 1953 when they began to engage in the process, though it was a half-hearted effort. The next two years they would begrudgingly go through the motions. The family was in a state of despair and shell shock. Upon hearing the news that her son was killed *after* the armistice, my mother's mom did not speak for six months. The fun-loving person known by everyone as Bunny turned morose and unresponsive. My grandfather became embittered and withdrew from the world. There was no light and no air. "Life was putting in your time until it was over. By the winter of 1957, me and your father had resigned ourselves that we were destined to be barren."

"Barren?" That hit me. It was the first time I had interrupted her. "Ma, barren?"

She went on to explain in substantial detail what it meant to have a void in your life, and why God decided to punish them to the point of incredulity. "We were good and decent people. Yes, we were little people, but we were hard-working, honest and thoughtful. He chose to take your uncle before Jackie had an opportunity to build his own life. We were destined, your father and I, to find our own way with little purpose."

Then came the phone call.

The Foundling Hospital was located on York Avenue and East 65th Street. This was the place where wayward women came to get themselves right with God and society.

The Catholic Church would take care of those who strayed from its teachings and begin them anew on a path toward righteousness. They worked in concert with the State of New York in placing bastards into proper Catholic homes. It was also free of charge.

"The Sister from the Foundling Home said, 'Come get your baby.' I hear that voice; I hear that voice as clear as I hear my own right now. Come get your baby. The phone fell out of my hand. Dad thought someone had died. I screeched at him 'We have our boy!' Your father welled up with tears. He picked up the phone and screamed into the receiver 'When do we come!?! When do we come?' The Sister stayed on with him and then with me for at least 20 minutes. We were …" She stopped mid-sentence.

My mom grabbed the used tissues she had placed on the TV tray. I went to the kitchen and brought her a box of Kleenex and placed it on the table.

"Thank you, dear. I'm ok."

"I know. I know you are." I took a beat and rose from the chair. "How about a drink?"

It is a safe bet to say I've spoken that four-word sentence more than any other phrase. The thousands of times I've used it as an ice breaker for guests, when I tended bar, out in the middle of the Indian Ocean on the equator during general quarters on the carrier, in the middle of mass …

before, during and after carnal relations, or to simply smooth over a tough situation. My folks were Irish. I was Irish. We drank.

"No, dear. Thank you."

"Really? Why not? I mean ..."

"No, dear. It's fine. Thank you. Let's just sit."

I refilled her water glass. As I sat back down, I looked into the spot where our mutt, Penny, used to have her food and water bowls.

"I miss Penny." It came out of me. I really did miss our dog, though. I wasn't attempting to make light or change the subject. It was a gut statement.

"Ed..." Another long pause. I mentally left the room. I came back. I lifted my head and nodded "I'm sorry."

"No. You don't have to be sorry. You don't have to be sorry for anything."

We looked at one another. No, it was more than looking. We focused on one another. It was the damndest thing. Something else came into the room. I don't know. The prism moved. The light shone differently. Both of us shifted. The person who I had known the longest, the individual with whom I was most familiar—there was more to her. There was more in the room. My God, look at this beautiful person.

"Your father and I were beyond ecstatic. We were over the moon. What we had dreamed about, what we had prayed for, this was actually happening. We would have our own baby, our very own child. This blessing came upon us from out of the blue. God was watching over us, and he said, 'here is your blessing.'"

She pointed her index finger in my direction. "Though I no longer attend church, and religion has turned against itself, I believe a higher power was looking after us."

My mother had grown to despise religion, and the Catholic Church in particular. Yes, our local priest did run off with the laic secretary. He had a change of heart. It happens. The problem was that he and his girlfriend had emptied the bank account established for the church's new annex. The hypocrisy was beyond the pale. Mom would keep God in her own way. Even after losing her brother to war, her husband to emphysema, and being forced out of her neighborhood, my mother had faith.

"We didn't want to say anything to anyone until you were home. When you did come home, all of our friends were ecstatic. I received so many baby clothes, I gave most of them to the Salvation Army. There was one overriding consideration. Neither of us realized that there would be a one-year probationary period. At any time, a social worker could knock on the door, unannounced, and ask us anything. Only once did they come by. Nice young woman. I walked her through the apartment. I heard the next day she inquired

91

about us through our neighbors. I believe they called your dad's employer once. For one year we were living on eggshells. I kept the apartment spotless. *Spotless.* I took you to the doctor every month for six months. Dr. Freud *(Dr. Freud?)* finally told me I had the healthiest baby in the Bronx and to please stop worrying."

She rearranged herself in the chair, extended her arms in my direction and then pulled them back. "Now ..." A stern smile took over her face. "Now, a year goes by. We get a call to come to the Bronx Courthouse to sign everything and to make it official. We go and sign. It's done. You belong to us. The agonizing, all the dread, is washed away. We have our boy." She took her hands, pantomiming a stack of documents, and placed the phantom documents on the TV tray. I'd never seen my mother do so much ad-libbing.

"We come home. You were asleep." She stated this in a whisper, as if, had I overheard them, I'd have called a lawyer. "We gathered all the paperwork and sat down in the kitchen. The both of us agreed that this would be the last day either of us would mention anything about the adoption. You were ours. That was it."

That *was* it. All papers were destroyed. No drama. The end.

I sat in the chair in a state of conscious numbness. Looking at the worn living room carpet, the pile had flattened on each side of the threshold. *Why the hell am I looking at the wall-to-wall carpeting?*

At this moment, all of my time and effort today was pointed toward my mom, making sure there was ease and contentment. My focus was on her. This had little to do with me. The only close family she had was Tammy and me. It was my responsibility to see she was safe. My adrenal glands were on overdrive. I didn't realize it at the time, but I was becoming emotionally spent. These last few hours had shaped up like a gothic novel, which is odd because I had never read a gothic novel.

"You mentioned all your friends. How about the neighbors? They must have been happy."

"Well, everyone kept to themselves, but yes, of course, everyone was pleasant and considerate. Grandpa and Grandma were very…"

I cut her off. "What about the Petersons?"

Mr. and Mrs. Bill and Helen Peterson lived in the same building as us, one floor up from my maternal grandparents. The Petersons would also move out to—you guessed it—Hopatcong, with their six kids. Their oldest, Barbara, took me and a bunch of neighborhood kids trick or treating one year. That was a memorable Halloween. I ate nearly every piece of candy given to me over a period of an hour, and subsequently threw up said candy over the course of the evening. The next time I saw Barbara, I was out of the Navy. Their fourth oldest, Bill, was in my grade, though he attended a different school. They had moved out of our apartment building a few years before us, and they arrived in town one year after us. In the summer of '69, a bunch of us were sitting around after playing baseball for hours, just throwing rocks and calling each other names. Someone mentioned they were from New York City, which wasn't unusual. White flight made most of the Jersey suburbs émigré destinations. Billy Peterson yelled out that he was from the Bronx. Hey, so was I.

"We didn't live far from Yankee Stadium!" He was so proud to claim his allegiance to the damn Yankees.

"Well, I'm a Met fan, and *we* lived close to the stadium too! MY grandfather worked for the Giants in the Polo Grounds!" I proudly shot back.

"Really. Yeah, well we lived right off of 161st Street."

"No kidding. So did I."

"Yeah, we lived on Melrose Avenue."

"What? Are you kidding?"

"Yeah. We were on 863 Melrose Avenue."

"Huh? What ... what did you say?"

We looked at one another as a couple of hikers reunited a long way from base camp.

"Wait a second…do you have an older sister named Barbara?"

"Hey, you're little Eddie Brady!"

"Oh man, you're Billy Peterson!" All the other guys were looking at us like we were aliens, the type of look you got as a character on the *Outer Limits* or *Twilight Zone*.

This interaction became the impetus for a rich, lifelong friendship. We became more than brothers. We got as close as two straight men can get without exchanging vows. When we reached our senior year, he was the tri-captain and quarterback on a two-win, seven-loss football team. I was the co-captain of the county-champion cross-country team (in high school, who would you rather be?). I got the lead in *Hello, Dolly*. He was Joe Handsome. I did the school's morning announcements and led the Pledge of Allegiance every morning over the PA system. He was Joe Handsome. I was his best man, he was mine. We have bared our souls to each other for over 50 years.

"So, Mr. and Mrs. Peterson have to know? How couldn't they?"

"My goodness, Ed. One day it was your father and me. The next day it was the three of us. We never made an announcement to the building; you didn't discuss and, certainly, you did not brag about family matters. Of course, they must have known."

95

My adrenal glands kicked back in. I got this odd mental image. Every morning when they arose, their first thought had to have been "Has Ed Brady found out he was adopted?" It ran through me like a skipped record. Whatever the algorithm that brought me to this thought, however the synapses got wired, my main concern, the only thought I had, was *I've got to let Mr. and Mrs. Peterson know that it's ok. I know everything. There is no need to worry.*

"Mom, I've got to let them off the hook." These poor people. All these years they have been carrying around this heavy onus. I must relieve them of this undue burden. They didn't ask for this. All six kids were long out of the house. They had been empty nesters for nearly a decade. Mr. Peterson was retired. Both of them enjoyed each other's company and liked having a serene and peaceful life. Mom was out of the emotional woods. The thought of possibly staying with her overnight now seemed unnecessary. There was no need for worry. The tough South Bronx babe I admired was a little shaken, but back on solid ground. *She's ok, so I'm good. Now, I've got to see the Petersons.*

I got up, put on my jacket, and for the third time in one day, got hugged like nobody's business.

"I love you, Edward. I love you more than anyone on this earth. Thank you, dear."

"Mom ..." I hugged my mother in a way which many would find uncomfortable. I squeezed her to the point where she let out a small grunt. She moved her hands from the top of my head and cradled my face. We looked at one another with fresh eyes.

It was a five-minute ride to the Petersons. I normally would come into someone's house with at least a six-pack, if not a cake or cookies or something. To hell with the cookies. I had to remove this burden, their burden. I was laser focused on alleviating their pain.

"Oh my God, Eddie Brady! How are you, hon?" Mrs. Peterson was always happy to see me. "Are you by yourself? Where's Tammy? How come the surprise? Come in. Come in."

Mr. Peterson was also happy to see me, though he'd never show it.

"Hey, what the hell are you doin' here? You lost?" The first thing he did was grab a cold beer from the fridge and place it in my hand. "If you need money, we don't have any."

Mrs. Peterson had a thing for owls. Figurines. Small, little watercolor paintings on the wall. A little goofy but nice. This was the first house where they had their own bedroom.

"So, how's work? Still in the city, right? Have you seen Bill and Michelle? What's new with you?"

"I just came from Mom's."

"How is she? I should give her a call. How's she doing?"

"Lovely lady, your mom. Her dad was a piece of work. Big Giants fan." Mr. Peterson would always mention my grandfather and the Giants.

"Well, I've got something to tell you."

"OH …" Mrs. Peterson became seriously concerned. "Is your mom alright? Are you ok?"

"No, no, please. Everybody is ok. We're all ok." I'd leave it to Mom to talk about her diagnosis. "I would like to tell you a story. It will take a few minutes."

"Did you get drafted by the Mets?" Mr. Peterson would take any opportunity to rib me about my team.

"Well … it's a little deeper than that …" Neither one of them had ever seen me this serious. They both sat straight up and looked at me dead on.

I began with the prior night's phone call. Matter of fact and to the point. I explained everything in minute detail. There was a point when Mr. Peterson began to sink into his chair, looking for an escape hatch. I attempted to be lighter in my delivery while keeping the message direct and without judgment. Mrs. Peterson did not budge. She was stoic and stern-faced. Not one movement, though her eyes were recording every word, like a stenographer in a courtroom.

I came to the end, letting them know Mom was sending her best this Thanksgiving, and that she was ok. I sat back in my chair, exhaled, and smiled.

"Well, isn't that interesting?" Mrs. Peterson gave the exact same response as my mom. The intonation was identical. The upward lilt on "interesting" was a carbon copy. Good Christ, I'm getting exhausted.

"Well ..." Mrs. Peterson collected herself. "Ed ... what does your mom say about all of this?"

"Ma'am, as I said, she confirmed everything."

"Well, then ... I, too, will confirm. Of course we knew."

Wow. That was painless. It's ok. I'm ok. They're ok. Everything is ok.

Mrs. Peterson rose from her chair and gave me a bear hug. She started on how happy they were for my folks, how my grandparents had transformed from introverts to extroverts overnight, describing how Bill, in his baby carriage, reached his hand out into my baby carriage. She was matter-of-fact about all of this. She was concerned for my mom but pleased that all was well.

"I got to hit the road. I'm going to go see Bill."

"Terrific!" She was relieved I wouldn't be alone. "That's a wonderful idea."

"Yeah. I'll tell him everything. This day has been full. I haven't had the chance to call him, but he needs to know."

"He needs to know …?" Mrs. Peterson shot back.

"I have to stop at our place and talk to Tammy. Please don't call him. I'll let him know in person."

Her face opened. "Oh, dear …" She placed her hands on my shoulders. "Dear, Bill knows. All my kids know."

The first time you get the wind knocked out of you, you're kind of suspended. I was nine or ten when I lost my grip swinging on a ten-foot-high bar and landed on my back. I was involuntarily looking at the sky from a prone position, not knowing how I got there. Oxygen left my body in a flash.

Bill knows, all my kids know.

Bill knows, all my kids know.

Bill knows, all my kids know.

I became translucent, invisible, removed. I checked-out emotionally. Through the years, I had heard of people having out-of-body experiences. These surreal events came from intellectuals and those in the know. This brought a smirk across my face, and a shrug of working-class disdain for those who knew better. Ohh … you don't understand. Really, it was a spiritual moment, it was other-worldly. *Yeah, and I'm Willie Mays. Get a grip. Get a job. Who the hell are you kidding?*

The look on my face gave Mrs. Peterson pause. It was the realization that she said too much too soon. I observed

100

the rose color leaving her face. She took a step back and placed her left hand to her mouth.

"Oh, dear, I'm sorry. I'm so sorry. Are you going …?"

"No, Mrs. Peterson, it's ok. Really, I'm fine."

I focused on one of her owl figurines. *A blue owl with red feathers?* As I placed my arm into my jacket sleeve, the scarf fell to the floor. We both reached down and hit our heads on each other's shoulders. The spontaneous laughter from the collision was a needed breather.

Mr. Peterson walked over to me and placed his hand straight out, his arm solid and stiff, and took hold of my right hand.

"Ed …"

That's all he could muster. "Ed." He looked at me with endearing concern. This gruff old Irishman couldn't say another word. He didn't have to.

I felt warm. The temperature rose. Mrs. Peterson presented the fallen scarf with what I would describe as a mother's smile. I clutched her hand and the scarf with what I believed to be a look of *I'm ok, you're ok.*

"Tell your mom we're thinking of her. I'll call her."

I traipsed down the steps to the front door. I made a point of forcing the screen door closed. The setting sun seemed brighter. *Damn, I'm warm.* As I removed the scarf from my neck, I heard that discernible whoosh when an inside door is thrown open. Mrs. Peterson was vigorously waving her hand, scratching her wedding band across the pane glass. Over her shoulder was Mr. Peterson, not so much waving but gesturing forward. I backed out of the driveway and took a glimpse at my buddy's parents, standing in their doorway, gazing at me with unquiet pride.

Turning off their road onto Santa Fe Trail, I became warmer. I was getting baked from the inside out. The car turned into an Amana oven. *No, no it wasn't. Stop. Just stop it. Please. The wise guy. Stop. Grip hold of yourself.*

They all knew.

My God man … This shit is actual. How can this …

How could she not tell me?!

Holy fuck, what the …

Why couldn't you tell me, Dad, goddamn, all those times out at the bar …

You couldn't tell me because …

Billy … not a word, nothing, silence all this time …

Son of a bitch. What the hell … NO, where the hell … why not …

Treating me like a fucking baby … goddamnit …

I've got to … the heat …

Nobody told me a thing … why the hell didn't they say …

The car maneuvered off onto a vacant lot, allowing traffic to pass. How did I get off the road? Autonomic reflex.

Get a grip. Get a hold of ...

There is more to surreal time. Past aggrieved confusion. Awake in dreamland. It all hit. It all hit me.

There is no measuring of emotion. The rush of fear overtaking the sense of well-being. Uncertainty over comfort. Unawareness over knowing. Taking for granted the everydayness, the banality of how you set and create your life is now placed onto an unseasoned landscape. No control, no say, no input for process.

I realized I was looking at the car's front license plate. The engine was running, and I was standing on the side of the road. The drops through the leafless trees. *I'm a foreigner. I've travelled this road thousands of times. On foot, bike, car. That's it. How is it that I feel I'm trespassing?*

We've all experienced not knowing where we are. The business trip, staying over at a friend's place. There is more than a moment when we need to gather our bearings and think where am I? There are the times of battling a hangover, attempts to regain memories of the previous evening, hoping to place a name with a scrawled phone number on a bar napkin.

This was ... unfamiliar.

To have a place of your own is a bedrock belief. Pull yourself up, work hard, create a sense of belonging. Look what is possible. I'm capable of achieving with this opportunity that is the USA. All that is needed is sweat and conviction. Anyone will achieve with dedication, hard work, goal setting. There is a place for you. The choices are abundant and there for the taking. The place you choose is your testament. This is my location. My family will place roots in this spot. This particular spot. We belong here. This is the reason *The Wizard of Oz* is the greatest film. It is about finding a place in the world you call your own. Creating the space, you'll have order. Comfort and ease will soon follow.

Twilight began. Jesus, it was nearly five. *Have I eaten anything today? I don't think so. Does it matter? Not really. Tammy first.* Driving the 45 miles back to Union City, my eyes were foggy. I was cognizant without concentration. The thought of my dad travelling this highway for oh so many years, leaving at 3:30 in the morning, driving five days, six days a week. I never heard him complain. Over a 120-mile round-trip commute, dealing with city traffic and 6 to 8 hours in a bread truck, for 15 years. Not one bitch. Nothing. I thought of all of my buddies' dads commuting to the city or Newark, realizing I never heard a gripe out of any of them. Towards the end, my dad may have made a side comment to my mom about the younger guys wanting his higher-commissioned routes. After he passed, my mom told me she pleaded with him to take the pension. He was worn down. The limp he garnered whilst playing stickball as a teenager, running into a fire hydrant at full speed, was now more pronounced. They had two and-a-half years of retirement time together and managed to get to the shore town of Spring Lake for a few long weekends. Neither one of them ever stepped foot on a plane. More often than not, she would see him peering out of the kitchen window, looking at nothing in particular, lost in his own home. He didn't know what to do with himself. The boredom challenged his sense of worth.

I arrived home, again. The sun had set. Only one of the driveway lights to our complex was up and running. There was a country feel to the place as I looked up to The Church of St. Michael the Archangel. Union City, the most densely populated town in the country at the time, gave off a bucolic vibe. Our living room shades were drawn open and the lights were on. I spotted the silhouette of Tammy coming down the stairs. I sat in our Chevy sedan, watching Tammy open the door, standing at the threshold and peering at me with those baby browns. As she was coming down the stairs, we were locked into a gaze of care, longing and straight-out empathy. The embrace we shared … Jesus, I don't know. We loved each other so much.

I conveyed in minute detail all of which transpired. As I peered into her eyes, her affect transformed into a sense of awed numbness. We had both had it. Exhausted and exhilarated. *This, whatever this is, isn't coming to pass ... it's here. A brand-new ballgame. No, no wait ... this isn't a game.*

So, what the hell is it?

We ambled up the stairs. "You feel like eating? Want a drink? How about going upstairs? Let's go upstairs ..." Her voice trailed off. My girl closed her eyes, and we caressed each other in a different way. The energy between us lit up the room. The simple act of cuddling, being with the one you love, more than resonates ... it's home.

"My God, Jesus." Making my way over to the couch I extended my hand to brace myself and collapse onto the cushions. Emotionally spent and in la-la land, I breathed deeply, gazed at Tammy, looked out the window, and then closed my eyes.

"I don't know ... I just ... I don't know how, um, uh ... what to do?"

My girl caressed my face, breathed deeply and sat next to me. There was an orderly affect about Tammy. "Tell me babe. Tell me everything."

In my third summation of the day, I started backwards with the visit to Bill's folks. "Poor Mr. Peterson. I made him uncomfortable in his own house. He wanted to disappear into his chair. Mrs. Peterson was pure stoicism. They were both lovely. Giving. They would have done anything I asked."

I looked past her as my voice trailed off. "Oh ..."

"Oh, and ..." Tammy waited for me to complete the sentence. I leaned back into the couch, opened my mouth to form some kind of word, closed my eyes and sat up.

"Bill knows."

"Bill knows what?"

"He knows everything."

"He knows ..." At this point Tammy went through an emotional metamorphosis from "huh?" to "I don't understand" to shock to "what the hell?" in three seconds. She looked, Jesus, the expression she gave I've never seen ... on anybody.

"Bill Peterson *knew?!?*"

"They all knew. His older sisters and his brothers. They all knew." Tammy was nuzzled next to me, and I made the statement not *to* her or *for* her benefit, simply a matter of record, of fact. They all knew, as if I informed her it was 40 degrees out.

Tammy caressed my thigh. "Bill has always known and said nothing? My God, that is remarkable. The whole family. Everybody ... and no one said anything." Her eyes filled up. "This is … my God. This is unbelievable. This is just unbelievable. I'm so …"

"Mr. Peterson would have killed him." It came out of me as simply as exhaling. He would have killed *them*.

"Well, yeah …" Silence. All I heard was the refrigerator motor going on. "And he woulda been right to do it."

"Yeah. Well, I guess, yeah he would have been … yeah."

Silence.

"I gotta go see him."

"See who?"

"Bill."

"When?" Tammy stroked my shoulder. "Not now?"

I half turned without looking at her. "Yeah. I mean, I can't leave him hanging. His mother had to have called him. I don't know. It's Saturday. They may not be in. I can't do this over the phone. I gotta go. I gotta see him face to face."

Tammy looked at me the way a mother looks at her 9-year-old son, knowing he has no athletic ability, watching him take the field, a combination of *you can do it kid/oh, you poor thing, what the hell are you going to do?*

"Go ahead babe, see him. I'm gonna lie down. I'm kinda beat. I don't know what the hell from … yet I'm …" Her voice trailed off.

Tammy wasn't searching for a word, she was spent, tired, emotionally drained. The battery was at zero. Her head rested into my sternum. The deep caress of my girl engulfed me and energized me all the same. How can this empty tank be energizing me?

"Honey, I'm sorry. Let's go upstairs. This has just ..."

"Go see Bill. Go. You *do* have to see him. He must have already talked to his folks. You can't let him ... you can't be ... please go see him. What the hell he must be doing ..."

"They're probably out. I don't know. They seem ..."

"Mrs. Peterson called him the second you left their house. You think they went out after speaking with her?" Tammy placed her hand to her lips. The quivering ran through her face. "Jesus, what do you think they think, er ... are thinking?"

"Honey ..." I stopped speaking. I sat there drifting. I sat there mulling. I sat there with no discernible point of focus. I was incoherent, and open-eyed. Buzzed without the imbibing. I was lost but at home. Oh, thank Christ for Tammy.

We were spread out on our oversized couch. There was this feeling of, well ... love making—the comfort and tenderness, with an odd contentment. We'd been separated the entire day, with mere spasms of touch. The day's

109

embraces of these three women left me emotionally filled as well as exhausted.

The strong pull to be with *my gal,* to simply collapse next to her …

"I gotta go. Somehow, I'd leave them out in the ether if I didn't show up. Hell, they'll probably …"

"He has to be concerned, worried. He's going through something … that … well he'd … Jesus. I don't know … maybe he's feeling lost. Afraid." We sat in stillness for three, four minutes. For the first time since we moved in, the new house became comfortable. The small sprinklings of sawdust on the banister and the faint odor of new carpet were now welcoming. Unfamiliarity faded away. The place became ours.

"Give them both my love. Maybe we'll have dinner. They should come here. Let's have dinner …"

It was early evening, though it felt like three in the morning. We deep kissed and hugged then as if one of us was flying off for three weeks. I watched her traipse up the stairs as I headed out on my fourth sojourn of the day. That was in November of 1990.

* * *

Working for a satellite company based out of northern Virginia in 1985, the once-a-month commute to our nation's capital became mundane and somewhat off putting. Washington, DC is imposing and sterile. The marble buildings left me cold, generating neither energy nor character. All sound bounced off the facades like when a hockey goalie swats at a puck. Staid and cold, uninviting, with no welcome mats to be found, useful though unalluring. The observation became clear: this is the perfect place for politicians. Why would anyone with a smidgen of empathy live here? Which brings me to my maternal grandmother ...

Born in 1903, Agnes Baldock was at one time a fun-loving, cherubic woman. Nicknamed Bunny for her easy-going demeanor and open presence, her devil-may-care attitude powered her through the Depression and two world wars. Being a seamstress in their cold-water flat not only gave her standing in the neighborhood, but a needed, albeit small, flow of income. She became the *de facto* town crier and part-time matchmaker amongst the newly arrived Germans and Poles, and she reveled in knowing everyone's business. This glowing manner died after losing her son in Korea. When she received the Western Union telegram in August of 1953, catatonia supplanted joy. What made this horrific news beyond unbearable was that Jackie was killed eight days after the armistice was signed. After Grandma passed in 1980, my

111

mother informed me that she would mumble to herself "I need to be interred with my baby." For weeks it was a constant refrain. As for my grandfather, he wouldn't allow any Army representatives into the funeral home. Conversations were non-existent. It took three-and-a-half years for either one of them to see a semblance of possibility.

When Dolores walked through my grandparents' door with me in her arms, she saw the color reemerge in her mother's face. The drinking subsided. There was a purpose in life. Once exhumed from her comatose state, she'd spin wonderful yarns, which became saltier after her third *Rye Presbyterian*. Her early 20th Century upbringing in the South Bronx involved an amalgam of working-class emigres. The eastern European women who populated her apartment building would regale her with stories from the old country in Yiddish and broken *Romansch*. The vernacular and word play of these chain-smoking yentas would put sailors to shame. As I observed the plain, white obelisks and statues, and cold, unwelcoming places of business that are DC, one tale was brought forth.

Two women sitting on the stoop of their building, one of them hears another woman complain (never a compliment or a positive notion) that her son is involved with gangsters and hoodlums, lowlifes with no character or dignity. Though he brings food and money into the apartment, he is doomed to be a *schtunk*. She curses his choice of friends and life in this god-awful country. Her friend drags on the end of a poorly rolled cigarette, flicks the remnants into the gutter and exclaims, "Vell, dahrlinka … at least he's not a politician."

Having a Friday afternoon off in our nation's capital, I'd have felt guilty to not partake in a museum. It was the spring of 1984. For no apparent reason other than to kill time, I found myself at the National Archives. As I wandered by the US Constitution, the thought that our family history, my record of military service, is located in the same edifice as the Declaration of Independence. That's cool. My grandparents and my great-grandparents share space in a building with the Bill of Rights. There's a process for unearthing ancestry, why not take advantage? Realizing I would need ancient information, the go-to person would be Mom.

"Hello, dear. How are you, Ed?" Her cadence, the smooth ever so slight lilt of her voice … then her intonation, firm and welcoming. At four years old, at twenty-eight years old, the sound is home.

"How are you, Mom? Do you have a few minutes?"

There was an amicable pattern to our conversations. The initial topic was what my father was doing and how he was feeling. Then the question, "What did you have for lunch or dinner?" It made no difference what time it was, or where in the world I might be. I learned to say *less than an hour ago*, lest I begin to collapse from malnutrition. Letting three hours go by without consumption was considered heresy.

"Do you have some time? This may take a bit."

"Is everything alright, dear?"

"Everything is fine. I'm in DC. I've got some time on my hands ..."

"Is our nation's capital as cold and unwelcoming in person as it is on television?"

The apple doesn't fall far ...

I described the museum in pedestrian terms. Its purpose was bookkeeping for the nation.

"I need some information about our past, our family tree. I'd like to find out where and when your grandparents came into Ellis ..."

"WHAT do you need to know THAT for?"

Damn. Where the hell did that come from? I looked at the telephone receiver, checking for gremlins.

"Oh, well ... um, I'm trying to ..."

"Eddie, what was your grandparents' name?" She yells indiscriminately at my father who, I assume, is somewhere within a half mile of her screech.

"Mom, listen ... it's not a necessity. Don't worry. I could probably find some information ..."

"No. I don't know. Your father doesn't know. It's not something we … it's not … we don't, we didn't keep track of records. The records … they are few and far between. No one really kept anything."

There was a long pause, maybe ten, twelve seconds.

"Oh …" I said.

"Well, what I mean to say, dear, is there wasn't good bookkeeping back in the day."

My mother began to hurriedly ad-lib her way through our family history. There was back and forth on the Bronx. Her mother, Agnes, knew little of her mother's past, to say anything of her grandparents. My father's oldest sister, Edna, was the chronicler of all things in the Brady past. That knowledge became a faint memory after her passing. Anyone of my heritage was inextricably tied to the Bronx. Tremont Avenue. Fordham Road. The Grand Concourse. There was emphasis on The Grand Concourse. More of a boulevard, the Concourse was the Park Avenue of the borough. No one walked on the Concourse without proper attire. When Uncle Nick and Aunt Edna managed to land a railroad apartment on 167th and the Concourse in the early 60's, the whole family felt uplifted into the middle class. This accomplishment belonged to everyone. That housewarming party was a graduation ceremony. They all made it to a place that, for so many years, seemed a million miles away. My mom let out a heavy sigh, accompanied by that sound when you exhale with your lips together. I felt her lifting the pedal off the gas. She came back to being her composed and welcoming self.

"There is so much, Ed, that is foreign to your father and me. The fact is we simply don't know. There was so much hardship, so much pain. There was a lot of probably not wanting to know, not wanting to go back into the past. There was just … it was so very … well …"

"Mom, it's fine. Don't worry. It's ok. I simply had never looked into our family history before. No problem. It's ok. This all started by trying to kill time. I'm uh … wanting to know a little about you and Dad. No big deal."

"Yes, dear. We love you more than anything. I understand your curiosity. Who wouldn't like to know a little about their past? Sure, I see that. It's … normal. We were more concerned about each other in the then-and-now. It was a different time."

"Yeah. Sure. Believe me, I get it."

"My father and I concentrated on you." Did she mean my dad or her dad? "We made sure all was safe and secure. Nothing was more important. Nothing was more important than the safety we created, being sure there was plenty on the table. Your father and I had been through so much. My God, we had been through so much heartache. When you came into our lives … life began. All was new. We were so happy when you were born. You were such a blessing. Your grandparents were born again. Their life became new. Everything became a joy …"

Jesus. All I asked for was a couple of names.

"Mom, I know. I love you, too."

"Let us know how you make out with the information at your disposal. Call me when you get back … to civilization."

"I'll keep you abreast. Give Dad a punch for me."

"Be safe. I love you very much."

"Love you too."

I stared at the C&P telephone sticker, wondering what the hell just happened.

This was the third instance.

* * *

"Always tell the truth. It's the easiest thing to remember."

Ricky Roma, *Glengarry Glen Ross*

Though we were four months apart in age, Bill always seemed four years older than me. The upper-middle class presentation he gave to everyone he met was demure and charming, above the South Bronx fray. As a high school freshman, he easily passed for 21. Confident to the point of brashness, his head was held high over his six-foot-two frame. Conveying an unspoken braggadocio, he always dated above and beyond his pedigree. His unique ability to not only summon but maintain discreteness in all manner of situations defied his age. He'd travel into Manhattan to meet urbane young women before his 16th birthday.

His better half, Michelle, had fair yet strong Romanesque features with a sultry shock of auburn hair. Bill not only married up; he enriched his life by a magnitude of ten. Mimi gave him sophistication and grace, attributes rarely glimpsed in rural New Jersey, not to mention Melrose Avenue. Their modest yet elegant Art Deco one-bedroom in the East 50's (in a doorman building) oozed a Nick and Nora Charles aura. Her success as a graphic designer and his as a director of operations gave them standing, which both of their families admired.

As I parallel parked, it hit me. It wasn't so much of a realization but a matter of fact: I have a kid brother and four younger sisters. I'm the oldest of six. I'm an only child who's the oldest of six. Bill is the fourth of six kids. We now have something else in common. Yeah, but I'm the oldest, though he's still older than me.

I haven't eaten all day.

Now is not the time for a slice.

Okay, relax. Breathe deep. New territory.

Why am I talking to myself?

This is your best buddy. All is cool.

How the hell is it cool? What are you thinking?

I'm drifting in lala land. I haven't thought for hours.

I've got five siblings. Five real blood, honest-to-God relatives.

It's fine.

What's fine? No, it's not *fine*. It's fucking ... Jesus, it's

...

Breathe.

Shut up, will ya? Breathe! Yeah, breathe, all will be fine by ...

Get a hold. Look around ... it'll be nice to see them.

I wonder if he told Michelle.

Sure he did. Why hold back?

Christ, he held it from me.

119

What if ... what if ... my mom knew that he knew ... that they all knew ...

How did he hold it in all these years?

Are you done ranting? Ask him. Why don't you ask your best friend?

How do you ask?

This ... all of this ... this concerns him.

The doorman helped to push the revolving door as you entered. This is one helluva job. This guy's responsibility is to assist where none is needed.

"Good evening, sir. How are you?"

I'm a fucking basket case, you nosey ying-yang. Like you give a shit.

"Good evening."

"Ronald at the desk will assist you."

Of course, I needed you to direct me to a place 12 feet away from your sentry post. Without your comprehensive guidance, I'd have walked through the paned glass."

"Good evening, sir. How are you?"

Sweet Jesus, mother ... son of a bitch. Help me get through this ...

"Good evening. Ed Brady for Mr. and Mrs. Peterson, please."

"Are they expecting you?"

I glared at him in a way a Rottweiler looks at a new mailman. Donald (or was it Ronald?) pushed the intercom button thrice. He looked at his compadre at the revolving door in case back-up was needed. I faintly heard Bill's voice through his phone. Thank Christ, they're home.

* * *

THE NEW YORK FOUNDLING HOSPITAL

590 Avenue of the Americas

New York, NY 10011

Re: 13258

Dear Mr. Brady,

Thank you for reaching out to The New York Foundling. As an adoptee, New York State prohibits the release of identifying information therefore a summary of your father's time here at The Foundling as well as a redacted copy of his medical record will be provided. Should you want a copy of his original birth certificate you would need to contact the Department of Health and Mental Hygiene. *(sic)*

Birth and Placement History:

You were born on March 2nd, 1957 at Metropolitan Hospital. You were admitted to our care on March 6th, 1957. On March 7th, 1957, you were baptized at St. Vincent Ferrer's Catholic Church by Rev. Thomas B. Kelly, O.P.

A month into placement your birth mother signed surrender

documents for your adoption to take place. On December 9th, 1958 your adoption took place at Surrogate's Court of Bronx County before the Honorable Christopher C. McGrath.

Birth Family History:

Your birth mother was born in 1935 in the Southwest part of the United States. She was of the Roman Catholic faith and was of Irish, French, German ancestry. She attended college for a few months. She was described as 5 feet 2 inches tall, normally weighing 145lbs., brown hair, hazel eyes, and a fair complexion. She entered the military and served for a few months but was released after being diagnosed with schizophrenia.

Your birth father was born in 1930. He was of the Jewish faith and Australian *(sic)* American. He was described as 6 feet 1 inch tall, heavy build, black hair, brown eyes with a fair complexion. He was in college and worked as a draftsman.

The couple met at a gathering and began a physical relationship. Your birth mother informed him of the pregnancy in which he stated that he could not marry her because of his Jewish faith.

Your maternal grandfather was 54 years old at the time of

your birth. He was a manager at an exterminating company.

Your maternal grandmother was born in 1902 and passed away when your birth mother was born.

Your birth mother had three brothers. Her 26-year-old brother worked at a chemical company and was married with 3 children residing in the Southwest. A 25-year-old brother worked for an airline and was married living in the Northeast. A 22-year-old brother worked as a taxi driver was married with one child living in the Southwest.

Your birth mother was raised by her grandmother until her father remarried when she was 8 years old.

There is no additional non-identifying information. Should you have any questions please feel free to contact me.

Best regards,
Supervisor, Adoption & Record Information

"We cannot choose our external circumstances, but we can always choose how we respond to them."

--Epictetus

In the hospital room, my mom was upright on the bed, though gazing at her feet. One of her nicer house dresses covered her hospital gown. She turned her head and raised her arm, placing it across her midsection. I was unaware of the word despondency, though I saw it in my mom's demeanor.

"Ed, I'm tired."

Damn.

That was it. It was the phrase that placed us on a new path. My God, she actually said it. It was more than my cue. Ever practical and succinct, my mother decided it was time. Enough. This was enough. By Labor Day of 1992, Dolores Brady had battled lung cancer for two and a half years. Overnight stays in the hospital extended to three or four days. The inability to consume plain, bland meals, having to ingest quick-and-ready-flavored oatmeal. Though ulcers removed nearly half of her stomach some 25 years ago, she would savor a well-prepared entrée. Jesus, she loathed the sight of those oatmeal packets. Cisplatin, VP-16, pain killers. So many damn prescriptions. Since her diagnosis, she went about herself with her usual dignity and aplomb.

Independent, with more than a vein of conviction, my mother never lowered her head. Though she was realistic, this wretched disease would not alter her way of being. Rising early, maintaining her home, reading, conversing with friends. Presenting her amiable and elegant self to visitors, that would, at times, astonish even me. Always organized and smartly dressed. The head scarves purchased with Tammy at the Clothing Barn were regal crowns from Hermès. Hair loss be damned.

Her smile was not forced, though it was an attempt to comfort me. Placing my hand on her forearm, I smiled back and began to state the words that did not signify defeat, the waving of the white flag, though it was plainly understood. She took a breath, and stated with conviction, "Let's go home."

Damn, she beat me to it.

We planned for this phase for nearly six months. Lining up assistance from neighbors, Visiting Nurse Service, hospice care home providers. Although she put up faint resistance, Dolores was calmed by our presence. Tammy and I moved into my childhood home.

Tammy and I were at our best during the last eight weeks of my mom's life. Long after our divorce in 1998, of all which transpired and what we accomplished, that was the time we shone brightest. There is an emotion brought forth, a sense of, well … higher worth when taking care of a loved one. Though numerous components of family life stem from unspoken transactional agreements, the three of us understood how we would move forward. Still, having chosen not to have a family of our own, this was virgin territory for us. There was such a heightened sense of the other. Giving of yourself. Though there was an underlying sadness to its outcome, everything else in our lives faded into a holding pattern.

Though my folks were tempered by outward appearance, they had a perpetual open-door policy. No matter the season, our home always had air, always had light. So many of Tammy's friends and mine considered 304 Durban Avenue a second home. My parents cherished giving of themselves. In the final weeks of her life, it was Dolores who accepted all that was given. Her ex-coworkers sent a floral arrangement every Tuesday. Our local pizza place dropped off a veal parmigiana dinner every Thursday. (Mom had the vegetables, I had the veal). My in-laws were so loving. They made homemade chicken broth and visited thrice weekly. Tammy's sisters would visit and stay, even after Mom nodded off. The relationship with our pharmacist went back 25 years. I had enough morphine sulfate to buy a Porsche.

We were one month along into Mom's hospice care. Though it was barely nine o'clock, Tammy hit the hay. We'd take turns staying up with her, for the simple reason that she knew someone was close by. We kept her bedroom door open, enabling her to see into the kitchen. She liked watching us putter.

I would peer into her bedroom, making sure she was comfortable. On this night, I took a folding chair into her room. Her left hand, the one with her wedding band, was partially uncovered. As I moved the blanket to cover her exposed arm, I placed my palm over her fingers. I gently rubbed away the cold. Her head turned toward me. I felt a short smile come over my face. She slowly opened her eyes; her hand gently caressed my thumb. I wanted to say something. The both of us knew how much we felt for each other. It wasn't necessary. Still … I wanted … I needed to say it.

"Thank you."

I didn't want to break into tears, though I felt my eyes well up. I'm glad I said it.

My mom turned her head toward the wall and then back to me, as if she was trying to attain momentum. She clutched my hand and gave me a soft and firm response.

"No," she brought her other arm out of the blanket and reached for my face, "no, my dear … thank you."

* * *

128

Having a friend from birth can create a sense of your metamorphosis. The hand movements, facial expressions, speech patterns have been processed and categorized. Our histories are self-confessed to the point of boredom.

Michelle will not like me popping in unannounced.

Tough.

Has she ever really liked me?

I'm beginning not to like you. Knock on the damn door.

Bill and I always greeted each other with direct eye contact and a firm handshake. To only offer a partial glance and give a dead-fish handshake was outright disrespectful. I gave Michelle a buss on the cheek. She was always decked out to the nines and gave off a sophisticated air of relevance. Mimi and I have known each other for nearly a decade, though we didn't hit it off at first. I got the vibe that she thought I was not of her betrothed's ilk. She would tell Bill that I was jovial to the point of annoyance, though I was warm and polite. I'd come to grow on her like a pesky English ivy.

As I sat down on the borderline-comfortable, chic half-couch, both of my dear friends knew something was amiss. Driving on fumes as I traversed the Saturday night traffic, I found another emotional gear. As I had steeled myself with Mom, I would enact a similar performance here on East 54th Street.

"I need to talk to the both of you. Pour yourselves a whatever and sit down."

I asked them if Mrs. Peterson had given them a call. No, she had not. Hmm … interesting. OK, I'll need to give them the *entire story*. After these laborious and remarkable 7-8 hours of discovery, embellishment was not on the docket. Straight and to the point. They were looking at a serious Ed Brady. A focused, emotionally exhausted, though determined Ed Brady. No veneer. This was new. I was a serious 33-year-old man.

Bill took great pride in being a half-step ahead. Always organized, never off kilter. Look knowing though curious. Inquire with calm and calculated certainty. Never let them know that you don't know.

Not today. As I went through the day's phenomena, I could see him become uncomfortable. There was a point during my monologue where I saw in his eyes that I wasn't fishing. Michelle was uneasy. This was not an attempt to trap him to give it up. They saw that I knew. It was out. No more secrets. The burden was laid down. The adopted boy from Melrose Avenue knew he was adopted.

Bill handed me a drink and stepped back for emphasis.

"I'm glad you finally know."

There you have it. No bolt of lightning. No marching bands. The secret, the big thing, the onus, the *holy shit, what the hell do I do if this happens or that happens, or he asks me this or his mom asks me whatever* …

Over.

There was relief. This facet, this event, the knowing-I know-that-you-don't-know has concluded its run.

OK. Well, um, yea, alright.

OK. Well, um, yea, alright.

Here's where the memory of the day ends. The rest of the time at their place, not a clue. The rest of the night, I have no idea what I did. Knowing Mimi, she certainly would have asked about my mom. We probably made plans for dinner the following week. At some point I drove home. At some point I collapsed into bed. At some point my beloved Tammy snuggled and embraced her bone-tired guy. At some point, Edward Michael John Brady fell asleep.

Postscript

Tammy and I separated and eventually divorced in 1998 on amicable and respectful terms. My birth mother, Mary, and I had a subdued yet cordial relationship. She passed in 2016. Irving Hauptman, my birth father, a decorated Korean War veteran, left us in 2006. My mother, Dolores, passed away in her sleep in 1992. My dad, Ed Brady, died in 1985. I miss them both deeply.

During the holidays of 2022, my siblings and I had a family gathering in central Texas; over 30 people were in attendance. I was related to all of them. Growing up, I had two second cousins whom I rarely saw. There's a great old Hebrew expression, "Man plans and God laughs." Damn straight. My sisters Alice, Carol, and Diane each have two kids; my sister Bernice and brother Ed each have three. Every one of my 12 nieces and nephews are gorgeous human beings, as are their parents.

My mother, Dolores, said to me soon after the phone call from my birth mother, "You know Ed, it's funny, in a way it's kind of surreal … God is taking me from you and at the same time he is giving you your sisters and your brother."

I am one fortunate sonofabitch.

Acknowledgments

Bill Peterson is not a childhood friend. He is not a lifelong friend. We are as close as two straight men can be without taking vows. He has always been here for me. He championed this project before it became a project. He will always be here for me.

Dr. Lois Holzman and Dr. Dan Friedman, remarkable developmentalists and authors, guided me through my early drafts. Their expertise and kindness spurred me on.

Thanks to Blaise Allysen Kearsley and Kim Kassnove for guiding me through the onerous and sometimes painful writing of my "shitty first draft."

Thank you to Caroline Donnola, my editor, who did the final cut and guided me through the complex challenges of publishing.

I want to give my deepest appreciation to Tammy Albanese for being by my side during the challenging day depicted in this memoir.

Alice. Bernice. Carol. Diane. Ed. Each one of you has given me the courage to be a better man. I love you.

This book does not exist without my better half, Marian Rich. She gave me the capacity to pour out my feelings and put them on paper. Your willingness to listen, to encourage me over the years … you are the most giving person I have ever known. My love, this book is for you.